SQL
Pocket Guide

THIRD EDITION

SQL
Pocket Guide

Jonathan Gennick

O'REILLY®

Beijing · Cambridge · Farnham · Köln · Sebastopol · Tokyo

SQL Pocket Guide, Third Edition
by Jonathan Gennick

Copyright © 2011 Jonathan Gennick. All rights reserved.
Printed in the United States of America.

Published by O'Reilly Media, Inc., 1005 Gravenstein Highway North, Sebastopol, CA 95472.

O'Reilly books may be purchased for educational, business, or sales promotional use. Online editions are also available for most titles (*http://my.safari booksonline.com*). For more information, contact our corporate/institutional sales department: (800) 998-9938 or *corporate@oreilly.com*.

Editor: Julie Steele
Copyeditor: Teresa Elsey
Production Editor: Teresa Elsey
Proofreader: Emily Quill
Indexer: Ellen Troutman Zaig
Cover Designer: Karen Montgomery
Interior Designer: David Futato
Illustrator: Robert Romano

Printing History:

March 2004:	First Edition.
April 2006:	Second Edition.
November 2010:	Third Edition.

ISBN: 978-1-449-39409-7

[LSI]   [2011-06-17]

1308068794

Contents

SQL Pocket Guide

Introduction

This book is an attempt to cram the most useful information about SQL into a pocket-size guide. It covers commonly used syntax for the following platforms: IBM DB2 Release 9.7, MySQL 5.1, Oracle Database 11g Release 2, PostgreSQL 9.0, and Microsoft SQL Server 2008 Release 2.

Not all syntax will work on all platforms, and some features may not be available in earlier releases of these products. Whenever possible, I've tried to note any product or release dependencies.

Organization of This Book

Topics are organized alphabetically, with many section names carefully chosen to correspond to relevant SQL keywords. For example, see "Inserting Data" on page 67 for help with the INSERT statement.

Platform notes

MySQL requires the leading parenthesis in a function invocation to immediately follow the function name. For example, upper (name) will generate an error message because of the space between upper and (name).

Conventions

The following typographical conventions are used in this book:

UPPERCASE
　　Indicates an SQL keyword

lowercase
　　Indicates a user-defined item in an SQL statement

Italic
　　Indicates emphasis or a new technical term

`Constant width`
　　Used for code examples and for in-text references to table names, column names, expressions, and so forth

`Constant width bold`
　　Indicates user input in input/output code examples

`Constant width italic`
　　Indicates an element of syntax you need to supply

[]
　　Denotes an optional element of syntax

{}
　　Denotes a required choice

|
　　Separates choices in syntax

Example Data

All example SQL statements in this book execute against a set of tables and data that you can download from this book's catalog page at *http://oreilly.com/catalog/9781449394097/*. Figure 1 illustrates the relationships between the core tables, which give information on waterfalls in Michigan's Upper Peninsula. Some examples also use tables based on or derived from those in Figure 1.

The terms *datum, zone, northing,* and *easting* refer to Universal Transverse Mercator (UTM) grid coordinates, such as those you might use with a topographical map or GPS device. For more, see *http://erg.usgs.gov/isb/pubs/factsheets/fs07701.html*.

Some SQL examples in this book use a pivot table, which is nothing more than a single-column table containing sequentially numbered rows—in this case, 1,000 rows. The name of the table is `pivot`. (Exceptions! In SQL Server, `pivot` is a reserved word, so the SQL Server example script creates the table as `pivvot`, with two *v*s. In the MySQL script, the table `dual` is named `duel`.)

Using Code Examples

This book is here to help you get your job done. In general, you may use the code in this book in your programs and documentation. You do not need to contact us for permission unless you're reproducing a significant portion of the code. For example, writing a program that uses several chunks of code from this book does not require permission. Selling or distributing a CD-ROM of examples from O'Reilly books does require permission. Answering a question by citing this book and quoting example code does not require permission. Incorporating a significant amount of example code from this book into your product's documentation does require permission.

We appreciate, but do not require, attribution. An attribution usually includes the title, author, publisher, and ISBN. For example: "*SQL Pocket Guide*, by Jonathan Gennick (O'Reilly). Copyright 2011 Jonathan Gennick, 9781449394097."

If you feel your use of code examples falls outside fair use or the permission given here, feel free to contact us at *permissions@oreilly.com*.

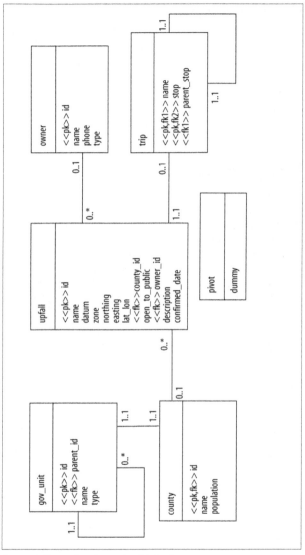

Figure 1. Example schema for this book

How to Contact Us

Please address comments and questions concerning this book to the publisher:

> O'Reilly Media, Inc.
> 1005 Gravenstein Highway North
> Sebastopol, CA 95472
> 800-998-9938 (in the United States or Canada)
> 707-829-0515 (international or local)
> 707-829-0104 (fax)

We have a web page for this book, where we list errata, examples, and any additional information. You can access this page at:

> *http://oreilly.com/catalog/9781449394097*

To comment or ask technical questions about this book, send email to:

> *bookquestions@oreilly.com*

For more information about our books, conferences, Resource Centers, and the O'Reilly Network, see our website at:

> *http://oreilly.com*

Safari® Books Online

Safari. Safari Books Online is an on-demand digital library that lets you easily search over 7,500 technology and creative reference books and videos to find the answers you need quickly.

With a subscription, you can read any page and watch any video from our library online. Read books on your cell phone and mobile devices. Access new titles before they are available for print, and get exclusive access to manuscripts in development and post feedback for the authors. Copy and paste code samples, organize your favorites, download chapters, bookmark key sections, create notes, print out pages, and benefit from tons of other time-saving features.

O'Reilly Media has uploaded this book to the Safari Books Online service. To have full digital access to this book and others on similar topics from O'Reilly and other publishers, sign up for free at *http://my.safaribooksonline.com*.

Acknowledgments

My heartiest thanks to the following people for their support, encouragement, and assistance: Grant Allen; Don Bales; Vladimir Begun; Tugrul Bingol; John Blake; Michel Cadot; Dias Costa; Chris Date; Bruno Denuit; Doug Doole; Chris Eaton; Stéphane Faroult; Iggy Fernandez; Bobby Fielding; Donna, Jenny, and Jeff Gennick; K. Gopalakrishnan; Jonah Harris; John Haydu; Kelvin Ho; Brand Hunt; Ken Jacobs; Chris Kempster; Stephen Lee; Peter Linsley; Jim Melton; Anthony Molinaro; Ari Mozes; Arup Nanda; Tanel Poder; Ted Rexstrew; Brandon Rich; Serge Rielau; Debby Russell; Andrew and Aaron Sears; Jeff Smith; Nuno Souto; Richard Swagerman; April Wells; and Fred Zemke.

Analytic Functions

Analytic function is Oracle's term for what the SQL standard refers to as a *window function*. See the section "Window Functions" on page 172 for more on this extremely useful class of function.

CASE Expressions: Simple

Simple CASE expressions correlate a list of values to a list of alternatives. For example:

```
SELECT u.name,
    CASE u.open_to_public
        WHEN 'y' THEN 'Welcome!'
        WHEN 'n' THEN 'Go Away!'
        ELSE 'Bad code!'
    END AS column_alias
FROM upfall u;
```

Simple CASE expressions are useful when you can directly link an input value to a WHEN clause by means of an equality condition. If no WHEN clause is a match, and no ELSE is specified, the expression returns null.

CASE Expressions: Searched

Searched CASE expressions associate a list of alternative return values with a list of true/false conditions. They also allow you to implement an IS NULL test. For example:

```
SELECT u.name,
    CASE
        WHEN u.open_to_public = 'y' THEN 'Welcome!'
        WHEN u.open_to_public = 'n' THEN 'Go Away!'
        WHEN u.open_to_public IS NULL THEN 'Null!'
        ELSE 'Bad code!'
    END AS column_alias
FROM upfall u;
```

Null is returned when no condition is TRUE and no ELSE is specified. If multiple conditions are TRUE, the first-listed condition takes precedence.

CAST Function

CAST explicitly converts a value to a new type. For example:

```
SELECT * FROM upfall u
WHERE u.id = CAST('1' AS INTEGER);
```

When converting from text to numeric or date types, CAST offers little flexibility in dealing with different input data formats. For example, if the value you are casting is a string, the contents must conform to your database's default text representation of the target data type.

NOTE

Most database brands have more useful conversion functions than CAST. SQL Server's CONVERT function is one such example. See the sections on Datetime Conversions and Numeric Conversions.

CONNECT BY Queries

Oracle Database supports CONNECT BY syntax for executing hierarchical queries. Beginning in Oracle Database 11g Release 2, you should consider the WITH clause, which in that release supports ISO standard syntax for recursive queries. See "Hierarchical Queries" on page 62.

NOTE

DB2 optionally supports CONNECT BY for compatibility with Oracle. There are some limitations, and support needs to be enabled through B2_COMPATI-BILITY_VECTOR.

Core CONNECT BY Syntax

To return data in a hierarchy, specify a starting node using START WITH, and specify the parent-child relationship using CONNECT BY:

```
SELECT id, name, type, parent_id
FROM gov_unit
START WITH parent_id IS NULL
CONNECT BY parent_id = PRIOR id;

ID    NAME        TYPE      PARENT_ID
----- ----------- --------- ---------
3     Michigan    state
2     Alger       county    3
1     Munising    city      2
4     Munising    township  2
5     Au Train    township  2
6     Baraga      county    3
7     Ontonagon   county    3
8     Interior    township  7
9     Dickinson   county    3
10    Gogebic     county    3
11    Delta       county    3
12    Masonville  township  11
...
```

The START WITH clause identifies the row(s) Oracle considers to be at the top of the tree(s). There is only one tree in this example, and it is for the state of Michigan. Alger County is a subdivision of Michigan. Munising and Au Train Townships are subdivisions of Alger County. Each entity's parent_id points to its enclosing entity.

Your START WITH condition does not necessarily need to involve the columns that link parent to child nodes. For example, use the following to generate a tree for each county:

```
START WITH type = 'county'
```

In a CONNECT BY query, the keyword PRIOR represents an operator that returns a column's value from either the parent or a child row, depending on whether you are walking the tree top-down or bottom-up. PRIOR is often used to define the recursive relationship, but you can also use PRIOR in SELECT lists, WHERE clauses, or anywhere else a column reference is valid.

Creative CONNECT BY

CONNECT BY is not limited to hierarchical data. Any data linked in a recursive fashion is a candidate for CONNECT BY queries. For instance, the tour stops in this book's example schema are linked in a fashion that CONNECT BY handles very well. The following query uses CONNECT BY to list each stop in its proper order:

```
SELECT t.name tour_name, t.stop
FROM trip t
START WITH parent_stop IS NULL
CONNECT BY parent_stop = PRIOR stop
       AND name = PRIOR name;
```

Because some waterfalls appear in more than one tour, CONNECT BY also includes a condition on tour_name to avoid loops. Output from the query is as follows:

```
TOUR_NAME   STOP
----------  ----------------------
M-28        3
M-28        1
M-28        8
M-28        9
M-28        10
M-28        11
Munising    1
Munising    2
Munising    6
Munising    4
Munising    3
Munising    5
US-2        14
US-2        12
US-2        11
US-2        13
```

You can also use CONNECT BY as a row generator. For example, to generate 100 rows (credit to Mikito Harakiri and Tom Kyte for showing me this clever trick), specify:

```
SELECT level x
FROM dual CONNECT BY level <= 100;
```

Some older releases of Oracle have a bug that you can avoid by placing the logic into a subquery:

```
SELECT x FROM (
    SELECT level x
    FROM dual CONNECT BY level <= 100);
```

You can also see the real-life case study "Finding Flight Legs" at *http://gennick.com/flight.html*.

WHERE Clauses with CONNECT BY

You can write WHERE clauses in CONNECT BY queries to restrict the results to specific rows of interest. The conditions in the CONNECT BY clause control which trees are processed by your query, and those trees in turn represent a candidate pool of rows. Conditions in the WHERE clause winnow down that candidate pool to only those rows that you wish the query to return.

Joins with CONNECT BY

A CONNECT BY query may involve a join, in which case the following order of operations applies:

1. The join is materialized first, which means that any join predicates are evaluated first.

2. The CONNECT BY processing is applied to the rows returned from the join operation.

3. Any filtering predicates from the WHERE clause are applied to the results of the CONNECT BY operation.

The following is an adaptation of the CONNECT BY query listing tour stops, which now incorporates a join to bring in the waterfall names:

```
SELECT t.name tour_name, t.stop, u.name falls_name
FROM trip t INNER JOIN upfall u
    ON t.stop = u.id
```

```
START WITH parent_stop IS NULL
CONNECT BY t.parent_stop = PRIOR t.stop
       AND t.name = PRIOR t.name;
```

Be careful! Don't write joins that inadvertently eliminate nodes from the hierarchy you are querying.

Sorting CONNECT BY Results

Oracle's CONNECT BY syntax implies an ordering in which, given a top-down walk of the tree, each parent node is followed by its immediate children, each child is followed by *its* immediate children, and so on. It's rare to write a standard ORDER BY clause into a CONNECT BY query, because the resulting sort destroys the hierarchical ordering of the data. However, beginning in Oracle9*i* Database, you can use the new ORDER SIBLINGS BY clause to sort each level independently without destroying the hierarchy:

```
SELECT id, name, type, parent_id
FROM gov_unit
START WITH parent_id IS NULL
CONNECT BY parent_id = PRIOR id
ORDER SIBLINGS BY type, name;
```

ID	NAME	TYPE	PARENT_ID
3	Michigan	state	
2	Alger	county	3
1	Munising	city	2
5	Au Train	township	2
4	Munising	township	2
6	Baraga	county	3

...

Baraga County follows Alger County because both are at the same level and Baraga County comes later in the sorting order. Within Alger County, the city is listed before the two townships because the sort is on **type** first, followed by **name**. The two townships are then sorted in alphabetical order. Each level in the hierarchy is sorted independently, yet each parent is still followed by its immediate children. Thus, the hierarchy remains intact.

Loops in Hierarchical Data

Hierarchical data can sometimes be malformed in that a row's child may also be that row's parent or ancestor. Such a situation leads to a *loop*. You can simulate a loop in the **trip** table by omitting AND **t.name** = PRIOR **t.name** from the CONNECT BY clause of the query to list tour stops. You can then detect that loop by adding NOCYCLE to the CONNECT BY clause and the CONNECT_BY_ISCYCLE pseudocolumn to the SELECT list:

```
SELECT t.name tour_name, t.stop,
       u.name falls_name, CONNECT_BY_ISCYCLE
FROM trip t INNER JOIN upfall u
    ON t.stop = u.id
START WITH parent_stop IS NULL
CONNECT BY NOCYCLE
    t.parent_stop = PRIOR t.stop;
```

NOCYCLE prevents Oracle from following recursive loops in the data. CONNECT_BY_ISCYCLE returns 1 for any row having a child that is also a parent or ancestor. Here are the preceding query's results:

```
TOUR_NAME STOP FALLS_NAME      CONNECT_BY_ISCYCLE
--------- ---- --------------- ------------------
Munising   1   Munising Falls   0
Munising   2   Tannery Falls    0
Munising   6   Miners Falls     0
Munising   4   Wagner Falls     0
Munising   3   Alger Falls      1
...
```

The 1 in the fourth column indicates that a loop arises from the node for stop 3. If you look carefully at the data in the **trip** table, you'll see two nodes where **stop** = 3. These nodes are for different tours. Without the restriction on **t.name**, one branch of recursive processing will go from stop 3 on the Munising tour to stop 1 on the M-28 tour (child of a stop 3) to stop 2 on the Munising tour (child of a stop 1). Eventually, you'll come again to stop 3 on the Munising tour, thereby creating the loop.

Supporting Functions and Operators

Oracle implements a number of helpful functions and operators to use in writing CONNECT BY queries:

CONNECT_BY_ISCYCLE
> Returns 1 when a row's child is also its ancestor; otherwise, it returns 0. Use with CONNECT BY NOCYCLE. (Oracle Database 10*g* and higher.)

CONNECT_BY_ISLEAF
> Returns 1 for leaf rows, 0 for rows with children. (Oracle Database 10*g* and higher.)

CONNECT_BY_ROOT(*column*)
> Returns a value from the root row. See PRIOR. (Oracle Database 10*g* and higher.)

LEVEL
> Returns 0 for the root node of a hierarchy, 1 for nodes just below the root, 2 for the next level of nodes, and so forth. LEVEL is commonly used in SQL*Plus to indent hierarchical results via an incantation such as the following:

```
RPAD(' ', 2*(LEVEL-1)) || first_column
```

PRIOR(*column*) *or* PRIOR *column*
> Returns a value from a row's parent. See also CONNECT_BY_ROOT.

SYS_CONNECT_BY_PATH (*column* , *delimiter*)
> Returns a concatenated list of *column* values in the path from the root to the current node. Each value is preceded by a *delimiter*, which you must specify as a string constant.
>
> Add SYS_CONNECT_BY_PATH(u.name,';') to the SELECT list of the tour query shown in "Joins with CONNECT BY" on page 11, and you'll get results such as these: ;Alger Falls, ;Alger Falls;Munising Falls, ;Alger Falls;Munising Falls;Scott Falls, and so forth. (Oracle9*i* Database and higher.)

Data Type Conversion

See the following topics for help on type conversion:

> CAST Function
> EXTRACT Function
> Datetime Conversions for your chosen platform
> Numeric Conversions for your chosen platform

Most platforms allow implicit conversion from one data type to another. Here's an example in Oracle:

```
SELECT * FROM upfall WHERE id = '1';
```

It's often better to use explicit type conversion so that you know for sure which value is getting converted and how.

Data Types: Binary Integer

Except for Oracle, the platforms support the following binary integer types:

> SMALLINT
> INTEGER
> BIGINT

These types correspond to 2-byte, 4-byte, and 8-byte integers, respectively. Ranges are –32,768 to 32,767; –2,147,483,648 to 2,147,483,647; and –9,223,372,036,854,775,808 to 9,223,372,036,854,775,807, respectively.

Data Types: Character String

For all platforms except Oracle, use the VARCHAR type to store character data:

```
VARCHAR(max_bytes)
```

MySQL allows TEXT as a synonym for VARCHAR:

```
TEXT (max_bytes)
```

In Oracle, append a 2 to get VARCHAR2:

```
VARCHAR2(max_bytes)
```

Oracle Database 9*i* and higher allows you to specify explicitly whether the size refers to bytes or characters:

```
VARCHAR2(max_bytes BYTE)
VARCHAR2(max_characters CHAR)
```

Using Oracle's CHAR option means that all indexing into the string (such as with SUBSTR) is performed in terms of characters, not bytes.

Maximums are 4,000 bytes (Oracle), 32,672 bytes (DB2), 8,000 bytes (SQL Server), 65,532 bytes (MySQL), and 1 GB (PostgreSQL).

Data Types: Datetime

Datetime support varies wildly among platforms; commonality is virtually nonexistent.

DB2

DB2 supports the following datetime types:

```
DATE
TIME
TIMESTAMP
TIMESTAMP(0to12default6)
```

DATE stores year, month, and day. TIME stores hour, minute, and second. TIMESTAMP stores both date and time, to a fractional position of up to 12 digits. The range of valid values is from 1 A.D. through 9999 A.D.

MySQL

MySQL supports the following datetime types:

```
DATE
TIME
```

```
DATETIME
TIMESTAMP
```

DATE stores dates from 1-Jan-1000 through 31-Dec-9999.
TIME stores hour/minute/second values from –838:59:59
through 838:59:59. DATETIME stores both date and time of
day (with the same range as DATE and TIME except that hours
max out at 23). TIMESTAMP stores Unix timestamp values.

The first TIMESTAMP column in a row is set to the current
time in any INSERT or UPDATE, unless you specify explicitly
a value of your own.

Oracle

Oracle supports the following datetime types:

```
DATE
TIMESTAMP
TIMESTAMP WITH TIME ZONE
TIMESTAMP WITH LOCAL TIME ZONE
TIMESTAMP(0to9default6) ...
```

DATE stores date and time to the second. TIMESTAMP adds
fractional seconds. WITH TIME ZONE adds the time zone.
WITH LOCAL TIME ZONE assumes each value to be in the
same time zone as the database server, with time zone trans-
lation taking place automatically between server and session
time zones. The range of valid datetime values is from 4712
B.C. through 9999 A.D. You can specify a fractional precision
of up to nine digits for any TIMESTAMP type.

PostgreSQL

PostgreSQL supports the following datetime types:

```
DATE
TIME [WITH[OUT] TIME ZONE]
TIMESTAMP [WITH[OUT] TIME ZONE]
TIME(0to6or0to10) ...
TIMESTAMP(0to6) ...
```

DATE stores a date only. TIME types store time of day. TIME-
STAMP types store both date and time. The default is to

exclude time zone. The range of years is from 4713 B.C. through 294,276 A.D. (TIMESTAMPs) and 5,874,897 A.D. (DATEs).

TIME and TIMESTAMP allow you to limit the number of precision digits for fractional seconds. The range depends on whether PostgreSQL stores time using a DOUBLE PRECISION floating point (0 to 6) or BIGINT (0 to 10). The default is DOUBLE PRECISION. The choice is a compile-time option. Using BIGINT drops the high end of the TIMESTAMP year range to 294,276 A.D.

SQL Server

SQL Server supports the following datetime types:

```
DATE
DATETIME
DATETIME2
DATETIME2(precision)
DATETIMEOFFSET
DATETIMEOFFSET(precision)
SMALLDATETIME
TIME
TIME(precision)
```

DATE stores date only from 1-Jan-0001 through 31-Dec-9999. DATETIME stores date and time of day to an increment of 3.33 milliseconds, with a range of 1-Jan-1753 through 31-Dec-9999. DATETIME2 is a combination of DATE and TIME. DATETIMEOFFSET extends DATETIME2 with a time zone offset. SMALLDATETIME stores date and time of day to the minute, with a range of 1-Jan-1900 through 6-Jun-2079. TIME stores time of day.

DATETIME2, DATETIMEOFFSET, and TIME take an optional parameter to specify the decimal precision of the seconds value. The default precision is to store seconds to seven decimal places. The valid range is from 0 through 7.

Data Types: Decimal

Decimal data types are rather more consistent across platforms than the datetime types. The following sections describe the more commonly used decimal types.

DB2's DECFLOAT Type

DB2 9.5 and higher support a new DECFLOAT type that is based on the IEEE 754r standard. DB2 supports two precision choices:

```
DECFLOAT(16)
DECFLOAT(34)
```

DECFLOAT(16) gives 16 digits of precision, requiring eight bytes of storage; DECFLOAT(34) gives 34 digits and requires 16 bytes of storage.

The range for DECFLOAT(16) is:

from $-9.999999999999999 \times 10^{384}$

to -1.0×10^{-383},

and from 1.0×10^{-383}

to $9.999999999999999 \times 10^{384}$.

The range for DECFLOAT(34) is:

from $-9.999999999999999999999999999999999 \times 10^{6144}$

to -1.0×10^{-6143},

and from 1.0×10^{-6143}

to $9.999999999999999999999999999999999 \times 10^{6144}$.

The DECFLOAT type supports five rounding modes:

ROUND_CEILING
> Rounds upward, always in a positive direction.

ROUND_FLOOR
> Rounds downward, always in a negative direction.

ROUND_HALF_UP
> Rounds to the nearest up or down value. Values of 0.5 round upward.

ROUND_HALF_EVEN
> Rounds to the nearest value. Values of 0.5 round up or down so as to make the final digit an even digit.

ROUND_DOWN
> Rounds toward zero.

You specify the rounding mode at the database level, using the parameter decflt_rounding. You must restart the database for any change to take effect.

DECIMAL/NUMBER Type

All platforms support the use of DECIMAL for storing numeric base-10 data (such as monetary amounts):

```
DECIMAL
DECIMAL(precision)
DECIMAL(precision, scale)
```

In Oracle, DECIMAL is a synonym for NUMBER, and you should generally use NUMBER instead.

DECIMAL(precision) is a decimal integer of up to precision dig-its. DECIMAL(precision, scale) is a fixed-point decimal number of precision digits with scale digits to the right of the decimal point. For example, DECIMAL(9,2) can store values up to 9,999,999.99.

Maximum *precision*/*scale* values are: 38/127 (Oracle), 31/31
(DB2), 38/38 (SQL Server), 65/30 (MySQL), and 1,000/1,000
(PostgreSQL).

Datetime Conversions: DB2

DB2 recently added a great deal of support to emulate Oracle's
TO_CHAR and TO_DATE functions. If compatibility with
Oracle is important, test to see whether the functions described
under "Datetime Conversions: Oracle" on page 28 will work
for you.

Otherwise, use the following functions to convert to and from
dates, times, and timestamps. In the syntax, *datetime* can be a
date, time, or timestamp; *date* must be either a date or a timestamp; *time* must be either a time or a timestamp; and *time
stamp* must be a timestamp. Similarly, *dateduration* must be a
date or timestamp duration; *timeduration* must be either a time
or timestamp duration; and *timestampduration* must be a timestamp duration. Valid string representations of all of these
types are allowed as well:

```
BIGINT(datetime)
CHAR(datetime, [ISO|USA|EUR|JIS|LOCAL])
DATE(date)
DATE(integer)
DATE('yyyyddd')
DAY(date)
DAY(dateduration)
DAYNAME(date)
DAYOFWEEK(date)
DAYOFWEEK_ISO(date)
```

```
DAYOFYEAR(date)
DAYS(date)
DECIMAL(datetime[,precision[,scale]]))
GRAPHIC(datetime, [ISO|USA|EUR|JIS|LOCAL])
HOUR(time)
HOUR(timeduration)
INTEGER(date_only)
INTEGER(time_only)
JULIAN_DAY(date)
MICROSECOND(timestamp)
MICROSECOND(timestampduration)
MIDNIGHT_SECONDS(time)
MINUTE(time)
MINUTE(timeduration)
MONTH(date)
MONTH(dateduration)
MONTHNAME(date)
QUARTER(date)
SECOND(time)
SECOND(timeduration)
TIME(time)
TIMESTAMP(timestamp)
TIMESTAMP(date, time)
TIMESTAMP_FORMAT(string, 'YYYY-MM-DD HH24:MI:SS')
TIMESTAMP_ISO(datetime)
TO_CHAR(timestamp, 'YYYY-MM-DD HH24:MI:SS')
TO_DATE(string, 'YYYY-MM-DD HH24:MI:SS')
VARCHAR(datetime)
VARCHAR_FORMAT(timestamp, 'YYYY-MM-DD HH24:MI:SS')
VARGRAPHIC(datetime, [ISO|USA|EUR|JIS|LOCAL])
WEEK(date)
WEEK_ISO(date)
YEAR(date)
YEAR(dateduration)
```

The following example combines the use of several functions to produce a text representation of confirmed_date:

```
SELECT u.id,
    MONTHNAME(u.confirmed_date) || ' '
|| RTRIM(CHAR(DAY(u.confirmed_date))) || ','
|| RTRIM(CHAR(YEAR(u.confirmed_date))) confirmed
FROM upfall u;
```

```
ID          CONFIRMED
----------- ---------------
          1 December 8,2005
          2 December 8,2005
          3 December 8,2005
          4 December 8,2005
```

Functions requiring date, time, or timestamp arguments also accept character strings that can be converted implicitly into values of those types. For example:

```
SELECT DATE('2003-11-7') ,
       TIME('21:25:00'),
       TIMESTAMP('2003-11-7 21:25:00.00')
FROM pivot WHERE x = 1;
```

Use the CHAR function's second argument to exert some control over the output format of dates, times, and timestamps:

```
SELECT CHAR(current_date, ISO),
       CHAR(current_date, LOCAL),
       CHAR(current_date, USA)
FROM pivot WHERE x=1;
```

```
2003-11-06 11-06-2003 11/06/2003
```

Use the DATE function to convert an integer to a date. Valid integers range from 1 to 3,652,059, where 1 represents 1-Jan-0001. The DAYS function converts in the reverse direction:

```
SELECT DATE(716194), DAYS('1961-11-15')
FROM pivot WHERE x=1;
```

```
11/15/1961      716194
```

Use the DECIMAL and BIGINT functions to return dates, times, and timestamps as decimal and 8-byte integer values, which will take the forms *yyyymmdd*, *hhmmss*, and *yyyymmddhhmmss.nnnnnnn*, respectively:

```
SELECT DECIMAL(current_date),
       DECIMAL(current_time),
       DECIMAL(current_timestamp)
FROM pivot
WHERE x=1;
```

```
20031106.  213653.  20031106213653.088001
```

The JULIAN_DAY function returns the number of days since 1-Jan-4713 B.C. (which is the same as 1-Jan in the astronomical year –4712), counting that date as day 0. There is no function to convert in the reverse direction.

Datetime Conversions: MySQL

MySQL implements a variety of datetime conversion functions, including some in support of Unix timestamps. The available functions are described in the following subsections.

Date and Time Elements

MySQL supports the following functions to return specific date and time elements:

```
DAYOFWEEK(date)
WEEKDAY(date)
DAYOFMONTH(date)
DAYOFYEAR(date)
MONTH(date)
DAYNAME(date)
MONTHNAME(date)
QUARTER(date)
WEEK(date)
WEEK(date, first)
YEAR(date)
YEARWEEK(date)
YEARWEEK(date, first)
HOUR(time)
MINUTE(time)
SECOND(time)
```

For example, to return the current date in text form, specify:

```
SELECT CONCAT(DAYOFMONTH(CURRENT_DATE), '-',
       MONTHNAME(CURRENT_DATE), '-',
       YEAR(CURRENT_DATE));
```

```
2-January-2004
```

For functions taking a *first* argument, you can specify whether weeks begin on Sunday (*first* = 0) or on Monday (*first* = 1).

TO_DAYS and FROM_DAYS

Use TO_DAYS to convert a date into the number of days since the beginning of the Christian calendar (1-Jan-0001 is considered day 1):

```
SELECT TO_DAYS(CURRENT_DATE);
```

    731947

Use FROM_DAYS to convert in the reverse direction:

```
SELECT FROM_DAYS(731947);
```

    2004-01-02

These functions are designed for use only with Gregorian dates, which begin on 15-Oct-1582. TO_DAYS and FROM_DAYS functions will not return correct results for earlier dates.

Unix Timestamp Support

The following functions convert to and from Unix timestamps:

UNIX_TIMESTAMP([*date*])

> Returns a Unix timestamp, which is an unsigned integer with the number of seconds since 1-Jan-1970. With no argument, you generate the current timestamp. The *date* argument may be a date string, a datetime string, a timestamp, or a numeric equivalent.

FROM_UNIXTIME(*unix_timestamp* [, *format*])

> Converts a Unix timestamp into a displayable date and time using the *format* you specify, if any. See Table 1 for a list of valid format elements.

For example, to convert 4-Jan-2004 at 7:18 PM into the number of seconds since 1-Jan-1970, specify:

```
SELECT UNIX_TIMESTAMP(20040104191800);
```

    1073261880

To convert that timestamp into a human-readable format, specify:

```
SELECT FROM_UNIXTIME(1073261880,
       '%M %D, %Y at %h:%i:%r');
```

```
January 4th, 2004 at 07:18:07:18:00 PM
```

The *format* argument is optional. The default format for the datetime given in this example is 2004-01-04 19:18:00.

Seconds in the Day

Two MySQL functions let you work in terms of seconds in the day:

SEC_TO_TIME(*seconds*)
> Converts seconds past midnight into a string of the form hh:mi:ss.

TIME_TO_SEC(*time*)
> Converts a time into seconds past midnight.

For example:

```
SELECT TIME_TO_SEC('19:18'), SEC_TO_TIME(69480);
```

```
69480    19:18:00
```

DATE_FORMAT and TIME_FORMAT

These two functions provide a great deal of flexibility in conversions to text. Use DATE_FORMAT to convert dates to text and TIME_FORMAT to convert times:

```
SELECT DATE_FORMAT(CURRENT_DATE,
       '%W, %M %D, %Y');
```

```
Sunday, January 4th, 2004
```

The second argument to both functions is a format string. Format elements in that format string are replaced with their respective datetime elements, as described in Table 1. Other text in the format string, such as the commas and spaces in this example, is left in place as part of the function's return value.

Table 1. MySQL date format elements

Specifier	Description
%a	Weekday abbreviation: Sun, Mon, Tue,...
%b	Month abbreviation: Jan, Feb, Mar,...
%c	Month number: 1, 2, 3,...
%D	Day of month with suffix: 1st, 2nd, 3rd,...
%d	Day of month, two digits: 01, 02, 03,...
%e	Day of month: 1, 2, 3,...
%f	Microseconds: 000000–999999
%H	Hour, two digits, 24-hour clock: 00...23
%h	Hour, two digits, 12-hour clock: 01...12
%I	Hour, two digits, 12-hour clock: 01...12
%i	Minutes: 00, 01,...59
%j	Day of year: 001...366
%k	Hour, 24-hour clock: 0, 1,...23
%l	Hour, 12-hour clock: 1, 2,...12
%M	Month name: January, February,...
%m	Month number: 01, 02,...12
%p	Meridian indicator: AM or PM
%r	Time of day on a 12-hour clock, e.g., 12:15:05 PM
%S	Seconds: 00, 01,...59
%s	Same as %S
%T	Time of day on a 24-hour clock, e.g., 12:15:05 (for 12:15:05 PM)
%U	Week with Sunday as the first day: 00, 01,...53
%u	Week with Monday as the first day: 00, 01,...53
%V	Week with Sunday as the first day, beginning with 01 and corresponding to %X: 01, 02,...53
%v	Week with Monday as the first day, beginning with 01 and corresponding to %x: 01, 02,...53
%W	Weekday name: Sunday, Monday,...

Specifier	Description
%w	Numeric day of week: 0=Sunday, 1=Monday,...
%X	Year for the week, four digits, with Sunday as the first day and corresponding to %V
%x	Year for the week, four digits, with Monday as the first day and corresponding to %v
%Y	Four-digit year: 2003, 2004,...
%y	Two-digit year: 03, 04,...
%%	Places the percent sign (%) in the output

Datetime Conversions: Oracle

You can convert to and from datetime types in Oracle by using the following functions:

```
TO_CHAR({datetime|interval}, format)
TO_DATE(string, format)
TO_TIMESTAMP(string, format)
TO_TIMESTAMP_TZ(string, format)
TO_DSINTERVAL('D HH:MI:SS')
TO_YMINTERVAL('Y-M')
NUMTODSINTERVAL(number, 'unit_ds')
NUMTOYMINTERVAL(number, 'unit_ym')

unit_ds ::= {DAY|HOUR|MINUTE|SECOND}
unit_ym ::= {YEAR|MONTH}
```

The *format* argument allows great control over text representation. For example, you can specify precisely the display format for dates:

```
SELECT name,
   TO_CHAR(confirmed_date, 'dd-Mon-yyyy') cdate
FROM upfall;

Munising Falls  08-Dec-2005
Tannery Falls   08-Dec-2005
Alger Falls     08-Dec-2005
...
```

And to convert in the other direction:

```
INSERT INTO upfall (id, name, confirmed_date)
VALUES (15, 'Tahquamenon',
        TO_TIMESTAMP('29-Jan-2006','dd-Mon-yyyy'));
```

Table 2 lists the *format elements* that you can use in creating a *format mask*. Output from many of the elements depends on your session's current language setting (e.g., if your session language is French, you'll get month names in French).

When converting *to* text, the case of alphabetic values, such as month abbreviations, is determined by the case of the format element. Thus, 'Mon' yields 'Jan' and 'Feb', 'mon' yields 'jan' and 'feb', and 'MON' yields 'JAN' and 'FEB'. When converting *from* text, case is irrelevant.

The *format* mask is always optional. You can omit it when your input value conforms to the default format specified by the following: NLS_DATE_FORMAT (dates) for dates, NLS_TIMESTAMP_FORMAT for timestamps, and NLS_TIMESTAMP_TZ_FORMAT for timestamps with time zones. You can query the NLS_SESSION_PARAMETERS view to check your NLS settings.

Table 2. Oracle datetime format elements

Element	Description
AM or PM	Meridian indicator.
A.M. or P.M.	
BC or AD	B.C. or A.D. indicator.
B.C. or A.D.	
CC	Century. Output-only.
D	Day in the week.
DAY, Day, or day	Name of day.
DD	Day in the month.
DDD	Day in the year.
DL	Long date format. Output-only. Combines only with TS.

Element	Description
DS	Short date format. Output-only. Combines only with TS.
DY, Dy, or dy	Abbreviated name of day.
E	Abbreviated era name for Japanese Imperial, ROC Official, and Thai Buddha calendars. Input-only.
EE	Full era name.
FF, FF1...FF9	Fractional seconds. Only for TIMESTAMP values. Always use two Fs. FF1...FF9 work in Oracle Database 10g and higher.
FM	Toggles blank suppression. Output-only.
FX	Requires exact pattern matching on input.
HH or HH12	Hour in the day, from 1–12. HH12 is output-only.
HH24	Hour in the day, from 0–23.
IW	ISO week in the year. Output-only.
IYY, IY, or I	Last three, two, or one digits of ISO year. Output-only.
IYYY	ISO year. Output-only.
J	Julian date. January 1, 4712 B.C. is day 1.
MI	Minutes.
MM	Month number.
MON, Mon, or mon	Abbreviated name of month.
MONTH, Month, or month	Name of month.
Q	Quarter of year. Output-only.
RM or rm	Roman numeral month number.
RR	Last two digits of year. Sliding window for hundreds value: 00–49 = 20xx, 50–99 = 19xx.
RRRR	Four-digit year; also accepts two digits on input. Sliding window just like RR.
SCC	Century. B.C. dates negative. Output-only.
SP	Suffix that converts a number to its spelled format.
SPTH	Suffix that converts a number to its spelled and ordinal formats.
SS	Seconds.

Element	Description
SSSSS	Seconds since midnight.
SYEAR, SYear, or syear	Year in words. B.C. dates negative. Output-only.
SYYYY	Four-digit year. B.C. dates negative.
TH or th	Suffix that converts a number to ordinal format.
TS	Short time format. Output-only. Combine only with DL or DS.
TZD	Abbreviated time zone name. Input-only.
TZH	Time zone hour displacement from UTC (Coordinated Universal Time).
TZM	Time zone minute displacement from UTC.
TZR	Time zone region.
W	Week in the month, from 1 through 5. Week 1 starts on the first day of the month and ends on the seventh. Output-only.
WW	Week in the year, from 1 through 53. Output-only.
X	Local radix character used to denote the decimal point. This is a period in American English.
Y,YYY	Four-digit year with comma.
YEAR, Year, or year	Year in words. Output-only.
YYY, YY, or Y	Last three, two, or one digits of year.
YYYY	Four-digit year.

Datetime Conversions: PostgreSQL

Convert between datetimes and character strings using the following functions:

```
TO_CHAR({timestamp|interval}, format)
TO_DATE(string, format)
TO_TIMESTAMP(string, format)
```

For example, to convert a date to the character representation of a timestamp, specify:

```
SELECT u.name,
       TO_CHAR(u.confirmed_date, 'dd-Mon-YYYY')
FROM upfall u;
```

```
    name       |   to_char
---------------+-------------
 Munising Falls | 08-Dec-2005
 Tannery Falls  | 08-Dec-2005
 Alger Falls    | 08-Dec-2005
...
```

To convert in the other direction (a character representation of a timestamp to a date), specify:

```
SELECT TO_DATE('8-Dec-2005', 'dd-mon-yyyy');
```

PostgreSQL closely follows Oracle in its support for format elements. Table 3 lists those available in PostgreSQL. Case follows form for alphabetic elements: use MON to yield JAN, FEB; Mon to yield Jan, Feb; and mon to yield jan, feb.

WARNING

You cannot apply TO_CHAR to values of type TIME.

You can also use TO_TIMESTAMP to convert a Unix epoch value to a PostgreSQL timestamp:

```
SELECT TO_TIMESTAMP(0);
```

Unix time begins at midnight, at the beginning of 1-Jan-1970, Coordinated Universal Time (UTC).

Table 3. PostgreSQL datetime format elements

Element	Description
AM or PM	Meridian indicator.
A.M. or P.M.	
BC or AD	B.C. or A.D. indicator.
B.C. or A.D.	

Element	Description
CC	Century. Output-only.
D	Day in the week.
DAY, Day, or day	Name of day.
DD	Day in the month.
DDD	Day in the year.
DY, Dy, or dy	Abbreviated name of day.
FM	Toggles blank suppression. Output-only.
FX	Requires exact pattern matching on input.
HH or HH12	Hour in the day, from 1–12. HH12 is output-only.
HH24	Hour in the day, from 0–23.
IW	ISO week in the year. Output-only.
IYY, IY, or I	Last three, two, or one digits of ISO standard year. Output-only.
IYYY	ISO standard year. Output-only.
J	Julian date. January 1, 4712 B.C. is day 1.
MI	Minutes.
MM	Month number.
MON, Mon, or mon	Abbreviated name of month.
MONTH, Month, or month	Name of month.
MS	Milliseconds.
Q	Quarter of year. Output-only.
RM or rm	Month number in Roman numerals.
SP	Suffix that converts a number to its spelled format (not implemented).
SS	Seconds.
SSSS	Seconds since midnight.
TH or th	Suffix that converts a number to ordinal format.
TZ or tz	Time zone name.
US	Microseconds.

Element	Description
W	Week in the month, from 1 through 5. Week 1 starts on the first day of the month and ends on the seventh. Output-only.
WW	Week in the year, from 1 through 53. Output-only.
Y,YYY	Four-digit year with comma.
YYY, YY, or Y	Last three, two, or one digits of year.
YYYY	Four-digit year.

Datetime Conversions: SQL Server

In SQL Server, you can choose one of four overall approaches to datetime conversion. The CONVERT function is a good general choice, although DATENAME and DATEPART provide a great deal of flexibility when converting to text.

CAST and SET DATEFORMAT

SQL Server supports the standard CAST function and also allows you to specify a datetime format using the SET DATEFORMAT command:

```
SET DATEFORMAT dmy
SELECT CAST('1/12/2004' AS datetime)

2004-12-01 00:00:00.000
```

For dates in unambiguous formats, you may not need to worry about the DATEFORMAT setting:

```
SET DATEFORMAT dmy
SELECT CAST('12-Jan-2004' AS datetime)

2004-01-12 00:00:00.000
```

When using SET DATEFORMAT, you can specify any of the following arguments: mdy, dmy, ymd, myd, dym.

CONVERT

You can use the CONVERT function for general datetime conversions:

```
CONVERT(datatype[(length)], expression[, style])
```

The optional *style* argument allows you to specify the target and source formats for datetime values, depending on whether you are converting to or from a character string. Table 4 lists the supported styles.

For example, you can convert to and from text:

```
SELECT CONVERT(VARCHAR,
            CONVERT(DATETIME, '15-Nov-1961', 106),
            106)

15 Nov 1961
```

Use the *length* argument if you want to specify the length of the resulting character string type. Subtract 100 from most style numbers for two-digit years:

```
SELECT CONVERT(DATETIME, '1/1/50', 1)

1950-01-01 00:00:00.000

SELECT CONVERT(DATETIME, '49.1.1', 2)

2049-01-01 00:00:00.000
```

SQL Server uses the year 2049 as a cutoff. Years 50–99 are interpreted as 1950–1999. Years 00–49 are treated as 2000–2049. You can see this behavior in the preceding example. Be aware that your DBA can change the cutoff value using the **two digit year cutoff** configuration option.

Table 4. SQL Server datetime styles

Style	Description
0, 100	Default: mon dd yyyy hh:miAM (or PM)
101[a]	USA: mm/dd/yyyy
102[a]	ANSI: yyyy.mm.dd
103[a]	British/French: dd/mm/yyyy
104[a]	German: dd.mm.yyyy
105[a]	Italian: dd-mm-yyyy
106[a]	dd mon yyyy
107[a]	mon dd, yyyy
108[a]	hh:mm:ss
9, 109	Default with milliseconds: mon dd yyyy hh:mi:ss: mmmAM (or PM)
110[a]	USA: mm-dd-yyyy
111[a]	Japan: yyyy/mm/dd
112[a]	ISO: yyyymmdd
13, 113	Europe default with milliseconds and 24-hour clock: dd mon yyyy hh:mm:ss:mmm
114[a]	hh:mi:ss:mmm with 24-hour clock
20, 120	ODBC canonical, 24-hour clock: yyyy-mm-dd hh:mi:ss
21, 121	ODBC canonical with milliseconds, 24-hour clock: yyyy-mm-dd hh:mi:ss.mmm
126	ISO8601, no spaces: yyyy-mm-yyThh:mm:ss:mmm
127	Time with time zone (literal T separating the date from the time): yyyy-mm-ddThh:mi:ss.mmm
130	Hijri: dd mon yyyy hh:mi:ss:mmmAM
131	Hijri: dd/mm/yyyy hh:mi:ss:mmmAM

[a] Subtract 100 to get a two-digit year.

DATENAME and DATEPART

Use the DATENAME and DATEPART functions to extract specific elements from datetime values:

```
DATENAME(datepart, datetime)
DATEPART(datepart, datetime)
```

DATENAME returns a textual representation, whereas DATEPART returns a numeric representation. For example:

```
SELECT DATENAME(month, GETDATE()),
       DATEPART(month, GETDATE())
```

```
January          1
```

Some elements, such as *year* and *day*, are always represented as numbers; however, the two functions give you the choice of getting back a string or an actual numeric value. Both of the following function calls return the year, but DATENAME returns the string '2004', whereas DATEPART returns the number 2004:

```
SELECT DATENAME(year, GETDATE()),
       DATEPART(year, GETDATE());
```

SQL Server supports the following *datepart* keywords: year, yy, yyyy, quarter, qq, q, month, mm, m, dayofyear, dy, y, day, dd, d, week, wk, ww, weekday, dw, hour, hh, minute, mi, n, second, ss, s, millisecond, ms, microsecond, mcs, nanosecond, ns, TZoffset, tz, ISO_Week, isowk, isoww.

DAY, MONTH, and YEAR

SQL Server also supports a few functions to extract specific values from dates:

```
DAY(datetime)
MONTH(datetime)
YEAR(datetime)
```

For example:

```
SELECT DAY(CURRENT_TIMESTAMP),
       MONTH(CURRENT_TIMESTAMP),
       YEAR(CURRENT_TIMESTAMP)
```

```
11            11           2003
```

Datetime Functions: DB2

DB2 implements the following *special registers* to return date-time information:

CURRENT DATE *or* CURRENT_DATE
> Returns the current date on the server.

CURRENT TIME *or* CURRENT_TIME
> Returns the current time on the server.

CURRENT TIMESTAMP *or* CURRENT_TIMESTAMP
> Returns the current date and time as a timestamp.

CURRENT TIMEZONE *or* CURRENT_TIMEZONE
> Returns the current time zone as a decimal number representing the time zone offset—in hours, minutes, and seconds—from UTC. The first two digits are the hours, the second two digits are the minutes, and the last two digits are the seconds.

DB2 also supports *labeled durations*. For example:

```
CURRENT_DATE + 1 YEARS - 3 MONTHS + 10 DAYS
```

Valid labels are YEAR, YEARS, MONTH, MONTHS, DAY, DAYS, HOUR, HOURS, MINUTE, MINUTES, SECOND, SECONDS, MICROSECOND, and MICROSECONDS.

NOTE

DB2 9.7 and higher now support many of the same functions as Oracle, notably: ROUND, TRUNC, ADD_MONTHS, LAST_DAY, NEXT_DAY, and MONTHS_BETWEEN. See "Datetime Functions: Oracle" on page 40 for details.

Datetime Functions: MySQL

MySQL implements the following functions to return the current date and time:

CURDATE() *or* CURRENT_DATE

> Returns the current date as a string ('YYYY-MM-DD') or a number (YYYYMMDD), depending on the context.

CURTIME() *or* CURRENT_TIME

> Returns the current time as a string ('HH:MI:SS') or a number (HHMISS), depending on the context.

NOW(), SYSDATE(), *or* CURRENT_TIMESTAMP

> Returns the current date and time as a string ('YYYY-MM-DD HH:MI:SS') or a number (YYYYMMDDHHMISS), depending on the context.

UNIX_TIMESTAMP

> Returns the number of seconds since the beginning of 1-Jan-1970 as an integer.

MySQL also implements the following functions for adding and subtracting intervals from dates.

DATE_ADD(*date* , INTERVAL *value units*)

> Adds *value* number of *units* to the *date*. You can use ADDDATE as a synonym for DATE_ADD.

DATE_SUB(*date* , INTERVAL *value units*)

> Subtracts *value* number of *units* from the *date*. You can use SUBDATE as a synonym for DATE_SUB.

For example, to add one month to the current date:

```
SELECT DATE_ADD(CURRENT_DATE, INTERVAL 1 MONTH);
```

Or, to subtract one year and two months:

```
SELECT DATE_SUB(CURRENT_DATE,
                INTERVAL '1-2' YEAR_MONTH);
```

Valid interval keywords for numeric intervals include SECOND, MINUTE, HOUR, DAY, MONTH, and YEAR. You can also use the string-based formats shown in Table 5.

Table 5. MySQL string-based interval formats

Keyword	Format
DAY_HOUR	'dd hh'
DAY_MINUTE	'dd hh:mi'
DAY_SECOND	'dd hh:mi:ss'
HOUR_MINUTE	'HH:MI'
HOUR_SECOND	'hh:mi:ss'
MINUTE_SECOND	'MI:SS'
YEAR_MONTH	'yy-mm'

Datetime Functions: Oracle

Oracle implements a wide variety of helpful functions for working with dates and times.

Getting Current Date and Time

It is common to invoke SYSDATE to return the current date and time in the server's time zone. For example:

```
SELECT SYSDATE FROM dual;

2006-02-07 09:32:32
```

You can use ALTER SESSION to specify a default date format for your session using the date format elements described in Table 2.

```
ALTER SESSION
    SET NLS_DATE_FORMAT = 'dd-Mon-yyyy hh: mi:ss';
```

The following Oracle functions return current datetime information:

CURRENT_DATE
    Returns the current date in the session time zone as a value of type DATE.

`CURRENT_TIMESTAMP[`*`(precision)`*`)]`

> Returns the current date and time in the session time zone as a value of type TIMESTAMP WITH TIME ZONE. The precision is the number of decimal digits used to express fractional seconds; it defaults to 6.

`LOCALTIMESTAMP[`*`(precision)`*`]`

> The same as CURRENT_TIMESTAMP, but it returns a TIMESTAMP value with no time zone offset.

`SYSDATE`

> Returns the server date and time as a DATE.

`SYSTIMESTAMP[`*`(precision)`*`]`

> Returns the current server date and time as a TIMESTAMP WITH TIME ZONE value.

`DBTIMEZONE`

> Returns the database server time zone as an offset from UTC in the form `'[+|-]hh:mi'`.

`SESSIONTIMEZONE`

> Returns the session time zone as an offset from UTC in the form `'[+|-]hh:mi'`.

Rounding and Truncating

Oracle allows you to round and truncate DATE values to specific datetime elements. The following example illustrates rounding and truncating to the nearest month:

```
SELECT SYSDATE, ROUND(SYSDATE,'Mon'),
       TRUNC(SYSDATE,'Mon')
FROM dual;

SYSDATE     ROUND(SYSDA TRUNC(SYSDA
----------- ----------- -----------
31-Dec-2003 01-Jan-2004 01-Dec-2003
```

Rounding is implemented to the nearest occurrence of the element you specify. My input date was closer to 1-Jan-2004 than it was to 1-Dec-2003, so my date was rounded up to the nearest month.

Truncation simply sets any element of lesser significance than the one you specify to its minimum value. The minimum day value is 1, so 31-Dec was truncated to 1-Dec.

Use the date format elements from Table 2 to specify the element for which you want to round or truncate a date. Avoid esoteric elements such as RM (Roman numerals) and J (Julian day); stick to easily understood elements such as MM (month), Q (quarter), and so forth. If you omit the second argument to ROUND or TRUNC, the date is rounded or truncated to the day (the DD element).

Other Oracle Datetime Functions

The following functions work with, and usually return, values of type DATE:

ADD_MONTHS(*date* , *integer*)
> Adds *integer* months to *date*. If *date* is the last day of its month, the result is forced to the last day of the target month. If the target month has fewer days than *date*'s month, the result is also forced to the last of the month.

LAST_DAY(*date*)
> Returns the last day of the month that contains a specified *date*.

NEXT_DAY(*date* , *weekday*)
> Returns the first specified weekday following a given *date*. The *weekday* must be a valid weekday name or abbreviation in the current date language for the session. (You can query NLS_SESSION_PARAMETERS to check this value.) Even when *date* falls on *weekday*, the function will still return the *next* occurrence of *weekday*.

MONTHS_BETWEEN(*later_date* , *earlier_date*)
> Computes the number of months between two dates. The math corresponds to *later_date* – *earlier_date*. The input dates can actually be in either order, but if the second date is later, the result will be negative.

The result will be an integer number of months for any case in which both dates correspond to the same day of the month, or for any case in which both dates correspond to the last day of their respective months. Otherwise, Oracle calculates a fractional result based on a 31-day month, also considering any time-of-day components of the input dates.

None of these functions is overloaded to handle TIMESTAMP values. Any timestamp inputs are converted implicitly to type DATE and consequently lose any fractional second and time zone information.

Datetime Functions: PostgreSQL

The following subsections demonstrate some of PostgreSQL's more useful datetime functions.

Getting Current Date and Time

PostgreSQL implements the following functions to return the current date and time:

```
CURRENT_DATE
CURRENT_TIME
CURRENT_TIMESTAMP
CURRENT_TIME [(precision)]
CURRENT_TIMESTAMP [(precision)]

LOCALTIME
LOCALTIMESTAMP
LOCALTIME [(precision)]
LOCALTIMESTAMP [(precision)]

NOW()
```

The function NOW() is equivalent to CURRENT_TIME-STAMP. The CURRENT functions return values with a time zone. The LOCAL functions return values without a time zone.

For example:

```
SELECT
    TO_CHAR(CURRENT_TIMESTAMP, 'HH:MI:SS tz'),
    TO_CHAR(LOCALTIMESTAMP, 'HH:MI:SS tz');
```

```
05:02:00 est | 05:02:00
```

Some functions accept an optional *precision* argument. You can omit the argument to receive the fullest possible precision. Alternatively, you can use the argument to round to *precision* digits to the right of the decimal. For example:

```
SELECT CURRENT_TIME, CURRENT_TIME(1);
```

```
17:10:07.490077-05 | 17:10:07.50-05
```

None of the previously listed functions advance their return values during a transaction. You will always get the date and time at which the current transaction began. The function TIMEOFDAY() is an exception to this rule:

```
SELECT TIMEOFDAY();
```

```
Sun Feb 05 17:11:39.659280 2006 EST
```

TIMEOFDAY() returns wall-clock time, advances during a transaction, and returns a character-string result.

Rounding and Truncating

PostgreSQL does not support the rounding of datetime values; however, it does provide a DATE_TRUNC function for truncating a datetime:

```
SELECT CURRENT_DATE,
       DATE_TRUNC('YEAR', CURRENT_DATE);
```

```
2006-02-05 | 2006-01-01 00:00:00-05
```

The result is either a TIMESTAMP or an INTERVAL, depending on what type of value is being truncated. The following are valid values for DATE_TRUNC's first argument: MICROSECONDS, MILLISECONDS, SECOND, MINUTE, HOUR, DAY, WEEK, MONTH, YEAR, DECADE, CENTURY, and

MILLENNIUM. Pass one of these values as a text string; case does not matter.

Other PostgreSQL Datetime Functions

Use AT TIME ZONE either to apply a time zone to a datetime without one or to convert a datetime from one time zone to another. For example:

```
SELECT CURRENT_TIMESTAMP;

 2006-02-05 17:28:38.534286-05

SELECT CURRENT_TIMESTAMP AT TIME ZONE 'PST';

 2006-02-05 14:28:38.541632
```

You can achieve the same results as those in the previous example through the TIMEZONE function:

```
SELECT TIMEZONE('PST', CURRENT_TIMESTAMP);
```

PostgreSQL supports an Ingres-inspired function called DATE_PART that provides the same functionality as the ISO-standard EXTRACT. For example, to extract the current minute value as a number, specify:

```
SELECT DATE_PART('minute', CURRENT_TIME);

 36
```

DATE_PART accepts all of the same datetime element names as EXTRACT. See "EXTRACT Function" on page 51.

Datetime Functions: SQL Server

SQL Server 2008 introduces a set of high-precision functions to return current datetime information:

SYSDATETIME()
　　Returns date and time as a DATETIME2 value.

`SYSDATETIMEOFFSET()`

> Returns date, time, and time zone offset as a DATETIMEOFFSET value.

`SYSUTCDATETIME`

> Returns current UTC time as a DATETIME2 value.

SQL Server continues to support the following functions from previous releases:

`CURRENT_TIMESTAMP` *or* `GETDATE()`

> Returns the current date and time on the server as a datetime value.

`GETUTCDATE()`

> Returns the current UTC date and time, as derived from the server's time and time zone setting.

SQL Server implements two functions for date arithmetic:

`DATEADD(datepart, interval, date)`

> Adds *interval* (expressed as an integer) to *date*. Specify a negative interval to perform subtraction. The *datepart* argument is a keyword specifying the portion of the *date* to increment, and it may be any of the following: `year`, `yy`, `yyyy`, `quarter`, `qq`, `q`, `month`, `mm`, `m`, `dayofyear`, `dy`, `y`, `day`, `dd`, `d`, `week`, `wk`, `ww`, `hour`, `hh`, `minute`, `mi`, `n`, `second`, `ss`, `s`, `millisecond`, `ms`. For example, to add one day to the current date, use `DATEADD(day, 1, GETDATE())`.

`DATEDIFF(datepart , startdate , enddate)`

> Returns *enddate – startdate* expressed in terms of the units you specify for the *datepart* argument. For example, to compute the number of minutes between the current time and UTC time, use `DATEDIFF(mi, GETUTCDATE(), GETDATE())`.

SQL Server 2008 introduces new functions to work with time zone offsets:

`SWITCHOFFSET(datetimeoffset, new_offset)`

> Inserts a new time zone offset into a DATETIMEOFFSET value and returns that new value.

```
TODATETIMEOFFSET(datetime2, new_offset)
```
Creates a DATETIMEOFFSET value from a DATETIME2 and an offset that you specify.

Specify time zone offsets in string form. For example, to convert the current time into U.S. Eastern Standard Time:

```
SELECT
  SWITCHOFFSET (
    SYSDATETIMEOFFSET(),
    '-05:00');
```

Negative offsets count westward from the prime meridian; positive offsets count eastward.

Deleting Data

Use the DELETE statement to delete rows from a table:

```
DELETE
FROM data_source
WHERE predicates
```

For example, you may want to delete states for which you don't know the population:

```
DELETE FROM state s
WHERE s.population IS NULL;
```

SQL Server, MySQL, and PostgreSQL 8.1 and earlier do not allow the alias on the target table. See the section "Predicates" on page 109 for more details on the different kinds of predicates that you can write.

Deleting in Order

MySQL requires that you include an ORDER BY clause in your DELETE statement when deleting multiple rows from a table having a self-referential foreign-key constraint. This is to ensure that child rows are deleted before their parents. Because MySQL checks for constraint violations *during* statement execution, this is a MySQL-only issue.

In the section "Subquery Inserts" on page 69, you will find an INSERT INTO...SELECT FROM statement that creates a new tour in the **trip** table called J's Tour. If you wish to delete J's Tour, you must issue a statement such as:

```
DELETE FROM trip WHERE name = 'J''s Tour'
ORDER BY CASE stop
        WHEN 1 THEN 1
        WHEN 2 THEN 2
        WHEN 6 THEN 3
        WHEN 4 THEN 4
        WHEN 3 THEN 5
        WHEN 5 THEN 6
        END DESC;
```

The CASE expression in this statement's ORDER BY clause hardcodes a child-first delete order. Obviously, this completely defeats the purpose of a multirow DELETE statement. If you're lucky, you'll have a sortable column that will yield a child-first delete order without its having to be hardcoded. In the case of this book's example schema and data, I wasn't so lucky.

Deleting All Rows

Omit the WHERE clause to remove all rows from a table:

```
DELETE FROM township;
```

Many database systems also implement a TRUNCATE TABLE statement that empties a table instantly, without logging, and thus with no hope of rolling back:

```
TRUNCATE TABLE township;
```

Oracle provides a form that preserves any space allocated to the table (which is useful if you plan to reload the table right away):

```
TRUNCATE TABLE township REUSE STORAGE;
```

Deleting from Views and Subqueries

All platforms allow deletes from views, but with restrictions. Oracle and DB2 allow deletes from a subquery (also known as an *inline view*). For example, to delete any states not referenced by the gov_unit table, you can specify:

```
DELETE FROM (
    SELECT * FROM state s
    WHERE s.id NOT IN (
        SELECT g.id FROM gov_unit g
        WHERE g.type = 'State'));
```

In PostgreSQL, a view that is the target of a DELETE must have an associated ON DELETE DO INSTEAD rule. PostgreSQL does not allow deleting from subqueries.

Various restrictions are placed on deletions from views and subqueries because, ultimately, a database system must be able to resolve a DELETE against a view or a subquery to a set of rows in an underlying table.

Returning Deleted Data: DB2

DB2 provides a very powerful option for retrieving the rows affected by a DELETE statement. Simply SELECT from the DELETE statement. For example:

```
SELECT * FROM OLD TABLE (
    DELETE FROM state
    WHERE name = 'Michigan'
);
```

Specify FROM OLD TABLE, and wrap your DELETE in parentheses.

Returning Deleted Data: Oracle

Oracle's solution to returning just-deleted rows is a RETURN-ING clause to specify the data to be returned and where it will be placed:

```
DELETE FROM  ...
WHERE  ...
RETURNING expression [,expression ...]
[BULK COLLECT] INTO variable [,variable ...]
```

For DELETEs of more than one row, the target variables must also be PL/SQL collection types, and you must use the BULK COLLECT keywords:

```
DECLARE
   TYPE county_id_array IS ARRAY(100) OF NUMBER;
   county_ids county_id_array;
BEGIN
   DELETE FROM county_copy
   RETURNING id BULK COLLECT INTO county_ids;
END;
/
```

Rather than specifying a target *variable* for each source *expression*, your target can be a record containing the appropriate number and type of fields.

Returning Deleted Data: SQL Server

SQL Server implements the OUTPUT clause for returning deleted rows from a query. For example:

```
DELETE FROM state
OUTPUT DELETED.id AS state_id,
       DELETED.name;
```

You can use the syntax OUTPUT DELETED.* to return all columns. You can specify expressions such as UPPER(DELETED.name). You can specify column aliases as in any query, with or without the optional AS keyword.

Double-FROM

SQL Server supports an extension to DELETE that lets you delete from a table based on values from a joined table. For example, to delete counties from `gov_unit` for which you do not know the population, specify:

```
DELETE FROM gov_unit
FROM gov_unit g JOIN county c
  ON g.id = c.id
WHERE c.population IS NULL;
```

The first FROM clause identifies the ultimate target of the DELETE. The second FROM clause specifies a table join. Then predicates in the WHERE clause can evaluate columns from both tables in the join. In this example, rows are deleted from the `gov_unit` table based on a corresponding population from the `county` table.

EXTRACT Function

DB2 (9.7 and higher), MySQL, Oracle, and PostgreSQL support the standard EXTRACT function to retrieve specific elements from a datetime value. In MySQL, for example:

```
SELECT EXTRACT(DAY FROM CURRENT_DATE);
```

The result will be a number. Valid elements are SECOND, MINUTE, HOUR, DAY, MONTH, and YEAR.

Oracle supports the following additional elements: TIMEZONE_HOUR, TIMEZONE_MINUTE, TIME-ZONE_REGION, and TIMEZONE_ABBR. The latter two Oracle elements are exceptions and return string values.

PostgreSQL also supports additional elements: CENTURY, DECADE, DOW (day of week), DOY (day of year), EPOCH (number of seconds in an interval, or since 1-Jan-1970 for a date), MICROSECONDS, MILLENNIUM, MILLISEC-ONDS, QUARTER, TIMEZONE (offset from UTC, in seconds), TIMEZONE_HOUR (hour part of UTC offset), TIMEZONE_MINUTE (minute part of offset), and WEEK.

GREATEST

DB2 (9.5 onward), MySQL, Oracle, and PostgreSQL implement the GREATEST function to return the largest value from
a list of values:

```
GREATEST(value [, value ...])
```

The input values may be numbers, datetimes, or strings. On
some platforms, if even one input value is null, then the function returns null.

Grouping and Summarizing

SQL enables you to collect rows into groups and to summarize
those groups in various ways, ultimately returning just one row
per group. You do this using the GROUP BY and HAVING
clauses, as well as various aggregate functions.

Aggregate Functions

An *aggregate function* takes a group of values, one from each
row in a group of rows, and returns one value as output. One
of the most common aggregate functions is COUNT, which
counts non-null values in a column. For example, to count the
number of waterfalls associated with a county, specify:

```
SELECT COUNT(u.county_id) AS county_count
FROM upfall u;
```

```
16
```

Add DISTINCT to the preceding query to count the number
of counties containing waterfalls:

```
SELECT COUNT(DISTINCT u.county_id)
       AS county_count
FROM upfall u;
```

```
6
```

The ALL behavior is the default, counting all values: `COUNT(expression)` is equivalent to `COUNT(ALL expression)`.

COUNT is a special case of an aggregate function because you can pass the asterisk (*) to count rows rather than column values:

```
SELECT COUNT(*) FROM upfall;
```

Nullity is irrelevant when `COUNT(*)` is used because the concept of null applies only to columns, not to rows as a whole. All other aggregate functions ignore nulls.

Table 6 lists some commonly available aggregate functions. However, most database vendors implement aggregate functions well beyond those shown.

Table 6. Common aggregate functions

Function	Description
`AVG(x)`	Returns the mean.
`COUNT(x)`	Counts non-null `values`.
`MAX(x)`	Returns the greatest value.
`MEDIAN(x)`	Returns the median, or middle value, which may be interpolated. (Oracle only.)
`MIN(x)`	Returns the least value.
`STDDEV(x)`	Returns the standard deviation. Use STDEV (only one D) in SQL Server.
`SUM(x)`	Sums all numbers.
`VARIANCE(x)`	Returns the statistical variance. Is an alias to VAR_SAMP in PostgreSQL, and to VAR_POP in MySQL. Use VAR in SQL Server.

GROUP BY

Aggregate functions come into their own when you apply them to groups of rows rather than to all rows in a table. To do this, use the GROUP BY clause. The following query counts the number of waterfalls in each of the predefined tours:

```
SELECT t.name AS tour_name, COUNT(*)
FROM upfall u INNER JOIN trip t
```

```
      ON u.id = t.stop
   GROUP BY t.name;
```

When you execute a query like this one, the result-set rows are
grouped as specified by the GROUP BY clause:

```
TOUR_NAME   FALL_NAME
----------  ---------------
M-28        Munising Falls
M-28        Alger Falls
M-28        Scott Falls
M-28        Canyon Falls
M-28        Agate Falls
M-28        Bond Falls

Munising    Munising Falls
Munising    Tannery Falls
Munising    Alger Falls
Munising    Wagner Falls
Munising    Horseshoe Falls
Munising    Miners Falls

US-2        Bond Falls
US-2        Fumee Falls
US-2        Kakabika Falls
US-2        Rapid River Fls
```

After the groups have been created, any aggregate functions are
applied once to each group. In this example, COUNT(*) is evaluated separately for each group:

```
TOUR_NAME   COUNT(*)
----------  ---------------
M-28        6
M-28
M-28
M-28
M-28
M-28

Munising    6
Munising
Munising
Munising
Munising
Munising
```

```
US-2        4
US-2
US-2
US-2
```

Any columns to which an aggregate function has not been applied are now "collapsed" into one value:

```
TOUR_NAME   COUNT(*)
----------  ---------------
M-28        6
Munising    6
US-2        4
```

In practical terms, this collapsing of many detail rows into one aggregate row means that you *must* apply an aggregate function to any column not listed in your GROUP BY clause.

NOTE

Grouping usually implies a limited sort operation to sort the rows into their groups.

Listing the Detail Values

Oracle implements the LISTAGG function to aggregate detail values for a column into a single value per group. The result is a delimited list of values. The following example extends the previous section's query to return a column named stop with a comma-delimited list of falls on a given tour:

```
SELECT t.name AS tour_name,
  LISTAGG (u.name, ',') WITHIN GROUP
  (ORDER BY u.name ASC) AS stop
FROM upfall u INNER JOIN trip t
  ON u.id = t.stop
GROUP BY t.name;


TOUR_NAME   STOP
----------  -----------------------------
M-28        Agate Falls,Alger Falls,Bond
            Falls,Canyon Falls,Munising
            Falls,Scott Falls
```

Munising	Alger Falls,Horseshoe Falls,Miners Falls,Munising Falls,Tannery Falls,Wagner Falls

The parameters to LISTAGG specify the column to aggregate and the delimiter to use in creating the list. The WITHIN GROUP keywords are mandatory. The ORDER BY clause in parentheses is also mandatory, and in this case it sorts the list alphabetically. You can sort the list on any detail column. For example, you can sort the list of falls in the stop column by u.confirmed_date, by u.lat_lon, and so forth.

Reducing the GROUP BY List

Sometimes you want to list a column in the SELECT list of a GROUP BY query without having to list that same column in the GROUP BY clause. In the following query, a given county number implies a county name:

```
SELECT c.id AS county_id,
       c.name AS county_name,
       COUNT(*) AS waterfall_count
FROM upfall u INNER JOIN county c
  ON u.county_id = c.id
GROUP BY c.id, c.name;
```

Rather than grouping by the c.id and c.name columns, it might be more efficient to group by the c.id column only, which yields a much shorter sort key. The grouping sort will potentially run faster and use less scratch space on disk. One approach to doing this is specified as follows:

```
SELECT c.id AS county_id,
       MAX(c.name) AS county_name,
       COUNT(*) AS waterfall_count
FROM upfall u INNER JOIN county c
  ON u.county_id = c.id
GROUP BY c.id;
```

This query drops c.name from the GROUP BY clause. To compensate for that, the query arbitrarily applies the MAX function to that same column in the SELECT list. Because all county names within a group of similar `c.id` values are the same, MAX can return only that one name.

Grouping Before the Join

The GROUP BY examples in the preceding section involve a join that is performed before the grouping operation. Using a subquery, it's possible to restate the query in a way that causes the join to occur *after* the aggregation instead:

```
SELECT c.id AS county_id,
       c.name AS county_name,
       agg.falls_count
FROM county c INNER JOIN (
   SELECT u.county_id, COUNT(*) AS falls_count
   FROM upfall u
   GROUP BY u.county_id) agg
ON c.id = agg.county_id;
```

The advantage here is that the join involves far fewer rows because the aggregation occurs prior to the join, not after it. Another advantage is a potential reduction in scratch disk and memory requirements, as the rows involved in the GROUP BY operation and subsequent aggregation do not include any data from the `county` table.

HAVING

The HAVING clause is used to place restrictions on the rows returned from a GROUP BY query. For example, to list only those tours having at least six stops, specify the following:

```
SELECT t.name AS tour_name, COUNT(*)
FROM upfall u INNER JOIN trip t
   ON u.id = t.stop
GROUP BY t.name
HAVING COUNT(*) >= 6;
```

Never put a condition in the HAVING clause that does not involve an aggregation. Such conditions are evaluated much more efficiently in the WHERE clause.

ROLLUP

The ROLLUP operation supported in DB2, MySQL, Oracle, and SQL Server generates a summary row for each group. For example, to roll up tour stops by county in DB2, Oracle, or SQL Server 2008, specify the following:

```
SELECT t.name AS tour_name,
       c.name AS county_name,
       COUNT(*) AS falls_count
FROM upfall u INNER JOIN trip t
     ON u.id = t.stop
   INNER JOIN county c
     ON u.county_id = c.id
GROUP BY ROLLUP(t.name, c.name);
```

Use the WITH ROLLUP syntax in MySQL or SQL Server 2005:

```
SELECT t.name AS tour_name,
       c.name AS county_name,
       COUNT(*) as falls_count
FROM upfall u INNER JOIN trip t
     ON u.id = t.stop
   INNER JOIN county c
     ON u.county_id = c.id
GROUP BY t.name, c.name WITH ROLLUP;
```

Following is the output from the preceding queries. The rows in boldface are generated as a result of using ROLLUP:

```
TOUR_NAME   COUNTY_NAME FALLS_COUNT
----------  ----------- -----------
M-28        Alger       3
M-28        Baraga      1
M-28        Ontonagon   2
M-28                    6
US-2        Delta       1
US-2        Gogebic     1
US-2        Dickinson   1
US-2        Ontonagon   1
US-2                    4
Munising    Alger       6
Munising                6
                        16
```

The GROUP BY operation generates the normal summary by tour and county. The ROLLUP operation adds in summaries for all other possible levels by tour name and for the entire set of rows. M-28's six stops, for example, comprise three stops in Alger County, two in Ontonagon County, and one in Baraga County. There are 16 tour stops total across all tours.

CUBE

CUBE takes things a step further. It generates summaries for all possible combinations of the columns you specify, as well as a grand total. The following is the CUBE version of the preceding section's ROLLUP query for DB2, Oracle, and SQL Server 2008, but restricted to the Munising tour:

```
SELECT t.name AS tour_name,
       c.name county_name,
       COUNT(*) AS falls_count
FROM upfall u INNER JOIN trip t
     ON u.id = t.stop
   INNER JOIN county c
     ON u.county_id = c.id
WHERE t.name = 'Munising'
GROUP BY CUBE(t.name, c.name);
```

MySQL 5.1 does not support CUBE. SQL Server 2005 requires the WITH CUBE syntax:

```
SELECT t.name AS tour_name,
       c.name AS county_name,
       COUNT(*) AS falls_count
FROM upfall u INNER JOIN trip t
     ON u.id = t.stop
   INNER JOIN county c
     ON u.county_id = c.id
WHERE t.name = 'Munising'
GROUP BY t.name, c.name WITH CUBE;
```

The results in DB2, Oracle, and SQL Server are the same:

TOUR_NAME	COUNTY_NAME	FALLS_COUNT
		6
	Alger	6
Munising		6
Munising	Alger	6

These results are only for the Munising tour. CUBE generates far more rows than ROLLUP does.

GROUPING SETS

Oracle, DB2, and SQL Server implement the GROUPING SETS function to let you specify the groupings that you want. For example:

```
SELECT t.name AS tour_name,
       c.name AS county_name,
       COUNT(*) AS falls_count
FROM upfall u INNER JOIN trip t
     ON u.id = t.stop
   INNER JOIN county c
     ON u.county_id = c.id
GROUP BY
   GROUPING SETS(t.name, c.name);
```

```
TOUR_NAME   COUNTY_NAME FALLS_COUNT
---------   ----------- -----------
Munising                6
M-28                    6
US-2                    4
            Delta       1
            Ontonagon   3
            Gogebic     1
            Baraga      1
            Alger       9
            Dickinson   1
```

This data is a subset of the results generated by CUBE, but if it's all you need, then using GROUPING SETS is more convenient.

Related Functions

The following functions are helpful when using CUBE, ROLLUP, and GROUPING SETS:

GROUPING(*column*)

Returns 1 if a null column value was the result of a CUBE, ROLLUP, or GROUPING SETS operation; otherwise, it returns 0. (DB2, Oracle, SQL Server.)

`GROUPING_ID(column , column , ...)`

Behaves similarly to GROUPING, but this generates a bit vector of 1s and 0s, depending on whether the corresponding columns contain nulls generated by an extended GROUP BY feature. (Available only in Oracle9*i* Database and higher.)

`GROUP_ID()`

Enables you to distinguish between duplicate rows in the output from CUBE, ROLLUP, and GROUPING SETS. The function returns 0 through *n*–1 for each row in a set of *n* duplicates. You can use that return value to decide how many duplicates to retain. Use `HAVING GROUP_ID()=0` to eliminate all duplicates. (Oracle only.)

Following is an example of the GROUPING function, using SQL Server's WITH CUBE syntax. The function returns a 1 whenever a null is the result of the CUBE operation.

```
SELECT  t.name AS tour_name,
        c.name AS county_name,
        COUNT(*) AS falls_count,
        GROUPING(t.name) AS n1,
        GROUPING(c.name) n2
FROM upfall u INNER JOIN trip t
     ON u.id = t.stop
   INNER JOIN county c
     ON u.county_id = c.id
WHERE t.name = 'Munising'
GROUP BY t.name, c.name WITH CUBE;
```

tour_name	county_name	falls_count	n1	n2
Munising	Alger	6	0	0
Munising	NULL	6	0	1
NULL	NULL	6	1	1
NULL	Alger	6	1	0

The n1 and n2 columns indicate when null tour and county names are the result of the CUBE operation rather than of data actually contained within the tables being queried.

Hierarchical Queries

DB2, Oracle, and SQL Server support the recursive use of WITH as defined in the ISO SQL standard for querying hierarchical and recursive data. PostgreSQL supports recursive WITH, but with a slight syntax difference.

NOTE

Oracle also supports a proprietary CONNECT BY syntax. See "CONNECT BY Queries" on page 8.

Recursive WITH

Following is an example recursive query that generates a hierarchical list of governmental units. States will be listed first, then counties, then townships.

```
WITH recursiveGov
    (depth, id, parent_id, name,
    type) AS
    (SELECT 1, parent.id, parent.parent_id,
            parent.name, parent.type
    FROM gov_unit parent
    WHERE parent.parent_id IS NULL
    UNION ALL
    SELECT parent.depth+1, child.id,
            child.parent_id, child.name,
            child.type
    FROM recursiveGOV parent, gov_unit child
    WHERE child.parent_id = parent.id)
SELECT depth, id, parent_id, name, type
FROM recursiveGOV;
```

PostgreSQL requires that you specify that the WITH clause is to be recursive by including the RECURSIVE keyword:

```
WITH RECURSIVE recursiveGov
...
```

Most of the preceding statement consists of a subquery named **recursiveGOV** that is specified using the WITH clause. The subquery consists of two SELECTs unioned together. Consider the first SELECT as the union query's starting point. It includes a predicate to treat rows having null `parent_id`s as the tree roots. Consider the second SELECT as defining the recursive link between parent and child rows.

The second SELECT brings in the children of the first. Because the second SELECT references the named subquery that it is part of (itself), it recursively brings back children of the rows it returned (and so forth until the end). The main SELECT kicks off all this recursion by simply selecting from the named subquery.

NOTE

For a more in-depth explanation of what happens when a recursive WITH executes, read the article "Understanding the WITH Clause" at *http://gennick.com/with .html*.

The output from the preceding query will look like this:

```
DEPTH ID PARENT_ID NAME     TYPE
----- -- --------- -------- --------
1     3            Michigan state
2     2  3         Alger    county
2     6  3         Baraga   county
...
```

Tracking Your Depth

To keep track of your depth in a hierarchy, create a `depth` column as shown in the example query. Have the first SELECT return 1 as the value for that column and have the second SELECT return `parent.depth+1`. Then the root node will be depth 1, the root's immediate children will be depth 2, and so on, down to the bottom of the hierarchy.

Breadth-First Versus Depth-First Sorting

Results are returned by default in the following breadth-first order, which differs from the order you'll get using Oracle's CONNECT BY syntax (described in "CONNECT BY Queries" on page 8):

1. The root node

2. The root's immediate children

3. The children of the root's immediate children

4. And so forth

Oracle lets you specify whether you prefer depth- or breadth-first sorting via a *search clause*. You can also specify how you want siblings ordered. Look at what follows the SEARCH keyword that precedes SELECT in the following example:

```
WITH recursiveGov
    (depth, id, parent_id, name,
     type) AS
    (SELECT 1, parent.id, parent.parent_id,
            parent.name, parent.type
     FROM gov_unit parent
     WHERE parent.parent_id IS NULL
     UNION ALL
     SELECT parent.depth+1, child.id,
            child.parent_id, child.name,
            child.type
     FROM recursiveGOV parent, gov_unit child
     WHERE child.parent_id = parent.id)
     SEARCH DEPTH FIRST
         BY name ASC NULLS FIRST
         SET ordering_column
SELECT depth, id, parent_id, name, type
FROM recursiveGOV
ORDER BY ordering_column;
```

You can specify either SEARCH DEPTH FIRST or SEARCH BREADTH FIRST. The preceding query returns results in depth-first order:

```
DEPTH ID PARENT_ID NAME      TYPE
----- -- --------- -------- --------
    1  3           Michigan  State
```

2	2 3	Alger	County
3	5 2	Au Train	Township
3	1 2	Munising	City

...

Key to these results is the SET ordering_column clause. That clause adds an extra column of output containing a value that you can sort on in the main query to ensure that rows are, in fact, returned in the specified breadth- or depth-first order. You can name the ordering column anything you wish. You can also include that column in your main query's select list, in the WHERE clause, and anywhere else in the main query a column name is allowed.

Detecting Recursive Loops

Oracle also supports syntax to detect loops in recursive data. For instance, the example data for this book has been carefully crafted to include a loop in the **trip** table. If you look closely at the raw data, you'll find that two stops share the same parent, leading to a loop. The following query uses the CYCLE clause to detect that problem and the resulting loop:

```
WITH recursiveTrip
    (name, stop, parent_stop)
AS (SELECT parent.name, parent.stop,
           parent.parent_stop
     FROM trip parent
     WHERE parent.parent_stop IS NULL
     UNION ALL
     SELECT child.name, child.stop,
            child.parent_stop
     FROM recursiveTrip parent, trip child
     WHERE child.parent_stop = parent.stop)
     SEARCH DEPTH FIRST
        BY stop ASC NULLS FIRST
       SET ordering_column
     CYCLE stop
       SET cycle_flag TO 'y' DEFAULT 'n'
SELECT name, stop, parent_stop, cycle_flag
FROM recursiveTrip;
```

A cycle in this case is any instance of a parent and child row sharing the same stop number. Hence the specification of

CYCLE stop in this query. The SET clause adds a new column to the query output, specifying that the column be set to y in the event that the row in question is the cause of a loop in the data. Here's what the output looks like:

```
NAME          STOP PARENT_STOP CYCLE_FLAG
----------    ---- ----------- ----------
Munising      1                n
Munising      2               1 n
Munising      6               2 n
Munising      4               6 n
Munising      3               4 n
M-28          1               3 y
Munising      5               3 n
...
```

If you omit the CYCLE clause and a loop results, Oracle will throw an ORA-32044: cycle detected while executing recursive WITH query error. When you specify both SEARCH and CYCLE clauses, you must specify them in that order. You can base loop-detection on a combination of multiple columns by specifying a comma-delimited list of columns following the CYCLE keyword.

Indexes, Creating

The basic CREATE INDEX statement syntax is:

```
CREATE INDEX falls_name ON upfall
   (name, open_to_public);
```

In this syntax, falls_name is the name of the index. The table to be indexed is upfall. The index is on the combined values of name and open_to_public.

Oracle and PostgreSQL allow you to assign an index to a tablespace:

```
CREATE INDEX falls_name ON upfall
   (name, open_to_public)
   TABLESPACE users;
```

Oracle and PostgreSQL also allow you to index column expressions:

```
CREATE INDEX falls_name ON upfall
    (UPPER(name), open_to_public);
```

This particular index is useful for resolving queries in which the WHERE clause predicates involve the expression UPPER(name).

Indexes on expressions are subject to various restrictions. SQL Server requires that such expressions return "precise" results, thus ruling out expressions returning or involving floating-point data types. Such expressions must also be deterministic, meaning that a given input *always* returns the same output, no matter the server or environmental settings.

Indexes, Removing

In DB2, Oracle, and PostgreSQL, you remove an index by naming it in a DROP INDEX statement:

```
DROP INDEX falls_name;
```

MySQL and SQL Server require you to also specify the table name:

```
DROP INDEX falls_name ON upfall;
```

Inserting Data

Use the INSERT statement to insert new rows in a table. You can insert one row, many rows, or the results of a subquery.

Single-Row Inserts

The following example adds a county to the gov_unit table. The values in the VALUES clause correspond to the columns listed after the table name:

```
INSERT INTO gov_unit
    (id, parent_id, name, type)
VALUES (13, 3, 'Chippewa', 'County');
```

Any columns you omit from an INSERT statement take on their default values specified at table-creation time. If you do not specify a default value at table-creation, then a null is used.

Use the DEFAULT keyword to specify explicitly that a column should take on its default value. Use the null keyword to insert a null value explicitly in a column that might otherwise default to a non-null value. For example:

```
INSERT INTO gov_unit
    (id, parent_id, name, type)
VALUES (14, DEFAULT, 'Mackinac', NULL);
```

If your VALUES list contains a value for each of the table's columns in the order specified at table creation, you can omit the column list:

```
INSERT INTO gov_unit
VALUES (15, DEFAULT, 'Luce', 'County');
```

For anything other than an ad-hoc insert (in other words, for inserts you embed in your scripts and programs), it's safer to specify a list of columns. Otherwise, such queries can fail the moment a new column is added to the target table.

Multirow Inserts

Many platforms provide the ability to insert multiple rows via repeated value lists in the VALUES clause:

```
INSERT INTO gov_unit
    (id, parent_id, name, type)
VALUES (16, 3, 'Menominee', 'County'),
       (17, 3, 'Iron', 'County'),
       (18, 3, 'Keweenaw', 'County');
```

Insert Targets

All platforms allow inserts into a view. DB2 and Oracle also allow inserts into subqueries (or inline views):

```
INSERT INTO
    (SELECT id, name, type FROM gov_unit)
```

```
    (id, name, type)
VALUES (19, 'Keweenaw', 'County');
```

PostgreSQL requires views that are the targets of inserts to have an associated ON INSERT DO INSTEAD rule.

Subquery Inserts

Using a subquery to feed an INSERT statement, it's possible to insert a number of rows at one time. For example, to create a duplicate of the Munising tour, but with a different name, specify:

```
INSERT INTO trip (name, stop, parent_stop)
    (SELECT 'J''s Tour', stop, parent_stop
     FROM trip
     WHERE name = 'Munising');
```

The SELECT statement in this form of INSERT must return an expression corresponding to each column listed after the target table. Some platforms let you get away without the parentheses surrounding the subquery, but it's safer to include them. The subquery can be any valid SELECT statement. It may return zero, one, or many rows.

MySQL requires that you sort your source rowset in a way that avoids loading any child row ahead of its parent. For example:

```
INSERT INTO trip (name, stop, parent_stop)
    (SELECT 'J''s Tour', stop, parent_stop
     FROM trip
     WHERE name = 'Munising'
     ORDER BY CASE stop
        WHEN 1 THEN 1
        WHEN 2 THEN 2
        WHEN 6 THEN 3
        WHEN 4 THEN 4
        WHEN 3 THEN 5
        WHEN 5 THEN 6
        END);
```

The issue with MySQL is that constraints are not checked at the end of a statement as in all other platforms, but rather they are checked as a statement executes—in this case, for each row inserted. Also, in this particular case, there is no column in the

trip table by which you can sort to prevent a constraint viola-
tion. Thus, you are forced to enumerate each row in the
ORDER BY clause, which virtually eliminates the benefit of
using INSERT INTO...SELECT FROM.

See the section "Deleting in Order" on page 47 for a DELETE
that will remove rows for **J's Trip** in the reverse order from
their insertion.

Returning Inserted Values: DB2

DB2 allows you to query newly inserted data by simply selecting from the INSERT statement. For example:

```
SELECT * FROM NEW TABLE (
   INSERT INTO gov_unit (id, name, type)
      VALUES (20, 'Limestone', 'Township')
);
```

Specify FROM NEW TABLE, and wrap your INSERT in
parentheses.

Returning Inserted Values: Oracle

Oracle supports a RETURNING clause to specify the data to
be returned and where it will be placed. The following example
works in Oracle SQL*Plus:

```
VARIABLE pid VARCHAR2(10);

INSERT INTO gov_unit (id, name, type)
   VALUES (19, 'Houghton', 'County')
   RETURNING parent_id INTO :pid;
```

VARIABLE is an SQL*Plus command used to create a bind
variable. This example returns one column. You can return
more than one column by simply separating column names and
result variables with commas:

```
RETURNING col1, col2  ...  INTO var1, var2 ...
```

See "Returning Deleted Data: Oracle" on page 50 for an example of the RETURNING clause showing the use of array
variables to return data from multiple rows.

Returning Inserted Data: SQL Server

You can use SQL Server's OUTPUT clause to return values from newly inserted rows. For example:

```
INSERT INTO gov_unit (id, name, type)
   OUTPUT INSERTED.parent_id AS pid
   VALUES (19, 'Houghton', 'County');
```

You can use the syntax `OUTPUT INSERTED.*` to return all columns. You can specify expressions such as `UPPER(INSERTED.name)`. You can specify column aliases as in any query, with or without the optional `AS` keyword.

Multitable Inserts

Using Oracle, you can issue INSERTs that affect multiple tables at once. You can insert the results of a subquery unconditionally into several tables, or you can write predicates that control which rows are inserted into which table. If you choose to write predicates, you can choose whether evaluation stops with one success or whether a row is considered for insertion into more than one table.

Unconditional multitable insert

Use INSERT ALL to insert the results of a subquery in more than one target table:

```
INSERT ALL
   INTO fall_description
      (id, name, description)
   VALUES (id, name, description)
   INTO fall_location
      (id, datum, zone, northing, easting)
   VALUES (id, datum, zone, northing, easting)
   SELECT id, name, description, datum,
          zone, northing, easting
   FROM upfall;
```

This example inserts location and description data in two separate tables. Different data is inserted in each table, but all data comes from the subquery. Each row returned by the subquery results in two new rows—one in each table.

Conditional multitable insert

Use WHEN clauses to insert conditionally in multiple tables. The following statement splits township and state data into two separate tables:

```
INSERT FIRST
WHEN type = 'Township' THEN
  INTO township (id, name)
  VALUES (id, name)
WHEN type = 'State' THEN
  INTO state (id, name)
  VALUES (id, name)
ELSE
  INTO other_unit (id, name)
  VALUES (id, name)
SELECT * FROM gov_unit;
```

The ELSE clause in this statement causes all rows that do not meet any other criteria to be added to the other_unit table. The ELSE clause is optional; you can omit it to ignore rows that do not meet at least one WHEN condition.

ALL versus FIRST

In a conditional multitable INSERT, the keyword ALL causes each row returned by the subquery to be evaluated against each WHEN clause. Thus, a row meeting criteria in two clauses can be inserted in more than one table. Use INSERT FIRST to stop evaluating a row after the first matching WHEN clause.

Joining Tables

Joins allow you to combine data from multiple tables into a single result-set row. There are two fundamental types of join: *inner* and *outer*. There are also two join syntaxes—the syntax introduced in the 1992 SQL standard, which depends on a JOIN clause, and an older syntax in which you separate table names with commas.

The Concept of a Join

The concept of a join is best explained by beginning with the earlier syntax. To join related rows from two tables, begin by listing two table expressions separated by a comma in your FROM clause. For example, to retrieve a list of waterfalls and their county names, you could begin by writing the following:

```
SELECT u.name AS fall, c.name AS county
FROM upfall u, county c;

FALL             COUNTY
---------------  ----------
Munising Falls   Alger
Munising Falls   Baraga
Munising Falls   Ontonagon
...
```

This result is a Cartesian product, which is all possible combinations of rows from the two tables. Conceptually, all joins begin as Cartesian products. From there, it's up to you to supply conditions to narrow down the results to only those rows that make sense. Using the older join syntax, you supply those conditions in the WHERE clause:

```
SELECT u.name AS fall, c.name AS county
FROM upfall u, county c
WHERE u.county_id = c.id;

FALL             COUNTY
---------------  ----------
Munising Falls   Alger
Tannery Falls    Alger
Alger Falls      Alger
...
```

These results are much more useful.

The process I've just described is purely conceptual; database systems will rarely or never form a Cartesian product when executing a join. However, thinking in these conceptual terms will help you write correct join queries and understand their results. Regardless of how the join operation is optimized, join results must match the conceptual results in the end.

Cross Joins

The SQL standard uses the term *cross join* to describe a Cartesian product. Generate a cross join as follows:

```
SELECT *
FROM upfall CROSS JOIN county;
```

One case in which cross joins *are* useful is when joining to a single-row result set. For example, to generate a report of tablespaces that include database_name, an Oracle database administrator could specify the following:

```
SELECT d.name database_name, t.name tablespace_name
FROM v$tablespace T CROSS JOIN v$database d;

DATABASE_NAME TABLESPACE_NAME
------------- -----------------------------
DB01          SYSTEM
DB01          UNDOTBS1
...
```

This cross join has the effect of replicating the v$database information to every row of the result set. Because there is only ever *one* row in v$database, the result set will still return one row per tablespace.

NOTE

DB2 began to support the CROSS JOIN syntax in release 9.5.

Cross joins are also useful in conjunction with DB2's LATERAL clause:

```
SELECT u.name, ings.direction, ings.meters
FROM upfall u,
     LATERAL (VALUES
                 ('Northing', u.northing),
                 ('Easting', u.easting))
     AS ings(direction, meters);
```

This query results in two rows per waterfall, one with the northing value and the other with the easting. For example:

```
NAME            DIRECTION METERS
--------------- --------- -----------
Munising Falls  Northing     5141184
Munising Falls  Easting       528971
Olson Falls     Northing     5140000
Olson Falls     Easting       528808
...
```

LATERAL generates a new table with values from the table to its left. The cross join expands each waterfall row into two rows.

Inner Joins

An *inner join* brings together corresponding rows from two tables. For example, you could list each waterfall in its corresponding county:

```
SELECT u.name AS fall, c.name AS county
FROM upfall u INNER JOIN county c
  ON u.county_id = c.id;
```

```
FALL            COUNTY
--------------- ----------
Munising Falls  Alger
Tannery Falls   Alger
Alger Falls     Alger
...
```

The keywords INNER JOIN between the two tables specify that the join should be an inner join. The ON clause specifies the *join condition*, or the condition that must apply in order for two rows to be considered related. Conceptually, as described in the preceding section, a Cartesian product is formed and the join condition is then applied to filter out unwanted combinations of rows.

The order of tables in an inner join is irrelevant. The INNER keyword is optional. A WHERE clause is still valid in join queries. For example, to report only on counties with a population above 10,000, use the following:

```
SELECT u.name AS fall, c.name AS county
FROM county c INNER JOIN upfall u
```

```
    ON u.county_id = c.id
  WHERE c.population > 10000;
```

Conceptually, the join results are materialized first, and the WHERE clause then restricts the results to those joined rows that satisfy the WHERE conditions. In reality, your database will find a more optimal approach to producing the results.

The USING Clause

MySQL, Oracle, and PostgreSQL support the USING clause. When the columns defining a join between two tables are identically named, and when the join condition would be an equality condition requiring that each set of identically named columns contain the same value (an *equi-join*), you can write the join more simply by replacing the ON clause with the USING clause. Here's an example:

```
SELECT *
FROM fall_description
JOIN fall_location USING (id);
```

There is a subtle issue to be aware of when using the USING clause. Consider the following query:

```
SELECT fd.id, fl.id
FROM fall_description fd
JOIN fall_location fl USING (id);
```

This version of the query will work in MySQL and PostgreSQL, but will fail in Oracle with the following error:

```
ORA-25154: column part of USING clause cannot have
qualifier
```

In Oracle, the USING clause merges the two id columns, and the result will have only *one* column named id (not fd.id and not fl.id). That column is associated with neither table, so neither table alias applies:

```
SELECT id
FROM fall_description fd
JOIN fall_location fl USING (id);
```

MySQL and PostgreSQL merge the two `id` columns into one (thus conforming to the ISO SQL standard), but they still allow you to select both an `fl.id` value and an `fd.id` value. However, a `SELECT *` against the join in MySQL or PostgreSQL will yield only one `id` column in the result.

Natural Joins

There is yet another shortcut beyond the USING clause, and that is the NATURAL JOIN syntax supported by MySQL, Oracle, and PostgreSQL. If two tables should be joined based on *all* columns they have in common with the same name and the join is an equi-join, you can use the NATURAL JOIN keywords without specifying explicitly the join conditions.

In Oracle, you cannot qualify a NATURAL JOIN column with an alias. For example, in the following query only one `id` column is returned, and it is not associated with either table (and hence not with any `fd` or `fl` alias):

```
SELECT id
FROM fall_description fd
NATURAL JOIN fall_location fl;
```

MySQL and PostgreSQL, on the other hand, give you the option to qualify join columns:

```
SELECT fd.id, fl.id
FROM fall_description fd
NATURAL JOIN fall_location fl;
```

Be wary of using NATURAL JOIN, especially in queries that you encapsulate within program code. The simple addition of a column to one table, if it has a name that happens to match a column in a joined table, can suddenly change the semantics of a NATURAL JOIN query. If you do use NATURAL JOIN, use it only for ad-hoc queries—and even then, be careful!

Non-Equi-Joins

So far, all the joins illustrated have been *equi-joins*, which involve corresponding columns from two tables that have the same values in two corresponding rows. Equi-joins are probably the most common type of joins, but it is sometimes useful and even necessary to write join conditions that are not equality-based. Such joins are sometimes referred to as *non-equi-joins*.

For example, the following statement creates a table of years via a subquery, and then it joins the table of months to upfall based on the value of upfall's confirmed_date. This particular example runs on MySQL, PostgreSQL and Oracle (because they support date literals):

```
SELECT u.name, y.year_num
FROM upfall u JOIN
(SELECT 2005 AS year_num,
        DATE '2005-1-1' AS year_begin,
        DATE '2005-12-31' AS year_end
 FROM dual
 UNION
 SELECT 2006 AS year_num,
        DATE '2006-1-1' AS year_begin,
        DATE '2006-12-31' AS year_end
 FROM dual) y
ON u.confirmed_date
BETWEEN y.year_begin AND y.year_end;
```

The result is an association of waterfalls to the year in which their data was confirmed:

```
NAME            YEAR_NUM
--------------- -----------------------
Munising Falls  2005
Tannery Falls   2005
Alger Falls     2005
...
Tahquamenon     2006
```

There are definitely easier ways to obtain this result, but this example does illustrate that not all joins need to be equi-joins.

Outer Joins

In an *outer join*, each row in the result set does not necessarily have to contain a row from both tables being joined; one or both tables are treated as optional. If you want a join to be done only when possible, and you want rows back regardless, use an outer join.

Left outer joins

Use a *left outer join* when you want all rows from one table, regardless of whether corresponding rows exist in the other table. Consider the possibility of a waterfall for which the owner is unknown: a row in `upfall` with a null `owner_id`. You want to list all waterfalls with their owners if possible, but even when no corresponding `owner` row exists, you still want to list *all* of the waterfalls. You can do that using a left outer join:

```
SELECT u.name AS fall, o.name AS owner
FROM upfall u LEFT OUTER JOIN owner o
  ON u.owner_id = o.id;

FALL             OWNER
---------------- ----------------
Miners Falls     Pictured Rocks
Munising Falls   Pictured Rocks
Tannery Falls    Michigan Nature
Tahquamenon
Rapid River Fls
Kakabika Falls
...
```

A left outer join designates the leftmost table as the *required table*. In this case, the leftmost table is the `upfall` table. Thus, each row in the final result from the query must correspond to a row from the `upfall` table. The `owner` table is the *optional table*. If an `owner` row exists that corresponds to a row from `upfall`, the result is the same as that from an inner join: a row with values from both tables. If no `owner` row corresponds to a given `upfall` row, a row is returned with data from `upfall`, but with nulls in place of all the `owner` values.

Interpreting nulls in an outer join

When interpreting the results from the left outer join in the preceding section, you can't really be certain that there is no owner listed for Kakabika Falls, for instance, because there could be an owner row but with a null name. A "safer" version of the query includes the primary key column from owner:

```
SELECT u.name AS fall, o.name AS owner, o.id
FROM upfall u LEFT OUTER JOIN owner o
  ON u.owner_id = o.id;
```

The o.id column is a primary key, meaning it cannot ever legitimately be null in the owner table. Therefore, if you see a null o.id value in the result of this query, you can rest assured that it is a result of the left outer join, not a result of finding a null in the corresponding owner row.

Another way to address the problem of interpreting an outer join is to always include the join columns in the result. If the join columns from the required table (e.g., u.owner_id) are not null, but the join columns from the optional table (e.g., o.id) are null, you have a case in which there is no corresponding row from the optional table (e.g., owner).

Right outer joins

A *right outer join* is the same as a left outer join except that the required table is the rightmost table—the second table to be listed. For example, the following two joins are semantically equivalent:

```
SELECT u.name AS fall, o.name AS owner
FROM upfall u LEFT OUTER JOIN owner o
  ON u.owner_id = o.id;
```

```
SELECT u.name AS fall, o.name AS owner
FROM owner o RIGHT OUTER JOIN upfall u
  ON u.owner_id = o.id;
```

In either case, **upfall** is the required table and **owner** is the optional table. The results of the two queries are identical. To avoid confusion between left and right, some SQL programmers write all such joins as LEFT OUTER JOINs.

Full outer joins

Sometimes you want an outer join in which both tables are optional. Such a join is a *full outer join*, and such joins are supported by DB2, Oracle, PostgreSQL, and SQL Server. You can write one as follows:

```
SELECT u.name AS fall, o.name AS owner
FROM upfall u FULL OUTER JOIN owner o
  ON u.owner_id = o.id;

FALL             OWNER
---------------  ---------------
Little Miners    Pictured Rocks
Agate Falls

                 Horseshoe Falls
```

This query returns falls without recorded owners and "owners" who own no waterfalls (i.e., potential owners), all in addition to the standard inner join results of falls and their corresponding owners.

Vendor-specific outer join syntax

In the past, database vendors have developed different ways to write outer joins. In Oracle, you used to identify the optional table by adding the suffix (+) to the optional table's column reference in all of the join conditions for the given join. For example:

```
SELECT u.name fall, o.name owner
FROM upfall u, owner o
WHERE u.owner_id = o.id(+);
```

Reversing the order of the columns in the predicate gives the same result. What matters is the location of the (+) operator:

```
SELECT u.name fall, o.name owner
FROM upfall u, owner o
WHERE o.id(+) = u.owner_id;
```

Older versions of SQL Server required the use of *= and =* in equality conditions to designate left and right outer joins, respectively. For example:

```
SELECT u.name fall, o.name owner
FROM upfall u, owner o
WHERE o.id *= u.owner_id;
```

Oracle and SQL Server still support these syntaxes (although in SQL Server, you must set your compatibility level to 80 or lower, using stored procedure **sp_dbcmptlevel**). However, your queries will be much easier to understand and debug if you write your joins using the JOIN clause.

LEAST

DB2 (9.5 onward), MySQL, Oracle, and PostgreSQL implement the LEAST function to return the smallest value from a list of values:

```
LEAST(value [, value ...])
```

The input values may be numbers, datetimes, or strings.

Literals

All database systems make provisions for embedding literal values in SQL statements. Text and numeric literals are usually quite simple, but there are some nuances of which you should be aware. Date and time literals tend to be more complex.

Text Literals

The ISO SQL standard for text literals is to enclose them in single quotes:

```
'This is a text literal'
```

Use two adjacent single quotes when you need to embed a single quote in a string:

```
'Isn''t SQL fun?'
```

SQL will treat the two adjacent single quotes as a single quote within the literal:

```
Isn't SQL fun?
```

Oracle Database 10g and higher allow you to specify alternative quoting delimiters, which are always two characters and always include leading and trailing single quotes. Introduce delimiters by prefacing them with a Q or a q. For example, to use '[and]' as delimiters, specify:

```
Q'[This isn't as bad as it looks]'
q'[This isn't as bad as it looks]'
```

The (, [, and { characters are special cases in that their corresponding closing delimiters must be),], and }, respectively. Otherwise, use the same character to close the string that you use to open it:

```
Q'|This string is delimited by vertical bars|'
```

You can't use space, tab, or return characters to delimit a string in this manner.

PostgreSQL allows you to specify alternative quoting delimiters using a dollar-sign syntax, producing a *dollar-quoted string constant*. For example:

```
$tag$This is a dollar-quoted string constant$tag$
```

Replace *tag* with any desired sequence of characters. Your quoting delimiter is then tag. If you like, you can even use $ $ without any intervening tag text. Escape sequences (see Table 7) do not have any effect in dollar-quoted string constants; they are treated as literal character sequences. $$\t$$ yields the string \t, not a tab character.

MySQL allows you to include the escape sequences shown in Table 7 in string literals. PostgreSQL allows the escape sequences shown in Table 8.

Table 7. MySQL string literal escape sequences

Escape	Description
\0	NULL character (ASCII zero)
\'	Single quote
\"	Double quote
\b	Backspace
\n	Newline
\r	Carriage return
\t	Tab
\z	ASCII 26 or the Ctrl-Z character
\\	Backslash
\%	Percent sign
_	Underscore

Table 8. PostgreSQL string literal escape sequences

Escape	Description
\b	Backspace
\f	Form feed
\n	Newline
\r	Carriage return
\t	Tab
\octal	Character corresponding to the given octal value
\xhexadecimal	Character corresponding to the given hexadecimal value
\\	Backslash

Numeric Literals

Numeric literals follow standard conventions for writing numbers:

```
123    123.45    +123    -123.45
```

Numbers written without a decimal point are generally treated as integers. Oracle allows for a trailing F, f, D, or d to indicate FLOAT or DOUBLE, respectively:

```
123D    123.45F    +123d    -123.45f
```

You can also use scientific notation to write floating-point constants:

```
123.45E+23    123.45e-23
```

These literals are interpreted respectively as 123.45×10^{23} and $123.45 \div 10^{23}$.

Datetime Literals

The SQL standard defines the following formats for date, time, and timestamp literals, with hours specified according to a 24-hour clock:

```
DATE 'yyyy-mm-dd'
TIME 'hh:mi:ss [{+|-}hh:mi]'
TIMESTAMP 'yyyy-mm-dd hh:mi:ss [{+|-}hh:mi]'
```

For example, the following specifications refer to 19-Dec-2005, 8:00 PM, and 8:00 PM U.S. Eastern Standard Time on 19-Dec-2005:

```
DATE '2005-12-19'
TIME '20:00:00'
TIMESTAMP '2005-12-19 20:00:00 -5:00'
```

SQL Server does not support these literals. DB2 does not support specifying the time zone.

Datetime Interval Literals

SQL defines the following formats for INTERVAL YEAR TO MONTH literals:

```
INTERVAL 'year-month' YEAR TO MONTH
INTERVAL 'year' YEAR
INTERVAL 'month' MONTH
```

Oracle9i Database and higher and PostgreSQL 9.0 and higher support these formats and also allow you to specify a precision for the year, which otherwise defaults to two digits:

```
INTERVAL '42-1' YEAR TO MONTH
INTERVAL '1042' YEAR(4)
```

Similarly, SQL defines the following formats for INTERVAL DAY TO SECOND literals:

```
INTERVAL 'dd hh:mi:ss.ff' DAY TO SECOND
INTERVAL 'hh:mi' HOUR TO MINUTE
INTERVAL 'mi' MINUTE
...
```

For an INTERVAL DAY TO SECOND literal, you can specify any contiguous range of time elements from days to seconds. In Oracle9i Database and higher, days (*dd*) and fractional seconds (*ff*) both default to two digits of precision.

Merging Data

DB2, Oracle, and SQL Server 2008 support the use of the MERGE statement for updating or inserting rows, depending on whether they already exist in the target table. For example, to merge potentially new waterfall data into the upfall table, specify the following:

```
MERGE INTO upfall u
USING (SELECT * FROM new_falls) nf
    ON (u.id = nf.id)
WHEN MATCHED THEN UPDATE
    SET u.name = nf.name,
        u.open_to_public = nf.open_to_public
```

```
WHEN NOT MATCHED THEN INSERT
    (id, name, datum, zone, northing, easting,
     lat_lon, county_id, open_to_public,
     owner_id, description, confirmed_date)
    VALUES (nf.id, nf.name, nf.datum, nf.zone,
        nf.northing, nf.easting, nf.lat_lon,
        nf.county_id, nf.open_to_public,
        nf.owner_id, nf.description,
        nf.confirmed_date);
```

This statement updates only `name` and `open_to_public` for existing waterfalls, although you could choose to update all columns if you wanted to do so. For new falls, all columns are inserted into the `upfall` table.

Oracle allows you to place WHERE conditions on both the UPDATE and INSERT operations. In addition, Oracle allows you to specify rows to be deleted *following* an UPDATE operation:

```
MERGE INTO upfall u
USING (SELECT * FROM new_falls) nf
    ON (u.id = nf.id)
WHEN MATCHED THEN UPDATE
    SET u.name = nf.name,
        u.open_to_public = nf.open_to_public
    WHERE nf.name IS NOT NULL
    DELETE WHERE u.open_to_public = 'n'
WHEN NOT MATCHED THEN INSERT
    (id, name, datum, zone, northing, easting,
     lat_lon, county_id, open_to_public,
     owner_id, description, confirmed_date)
    VALUES (nf.id, nf.name, nf.datum, nf.zone,
        nf.northing, nf.easting, nf.lat_lon,
        nf.county_id, nf.open_to_public,
        nf.owner_id, nf.description,
        nf.confirmed_date)
    WHERE nf.open_to_public = 'y';
```

This statement uses `WHERE nf.name IS NOT NULL` to prevent updating any name to a null. The subsequent DELETE WHERE clause then deletes any updated rows that no longer represent publicly accessible falls.

In DB2, you can specify a DELETE as the statement for a WHEN MATCHED clause. DB2 also allows more than one occurrence of the WHEN MATCHED and WHEN NOT MATCHED clauses. Following is the DB2 version of the preceding MERGE statement:

```
MERGE INTO upfall u
    USING (SELECT * FROM new_falls) nf
      ON (u.id = nf.id)
    WHEN MATCHED AND nf.name IS NOT NULL THEN UPDATE
      SET u.name = nf.name,
          u.open_to_public = nf.open_to_public
    WHEN MATCHED AND u.open_to_public = 'n' THEN DELETE
    WHEN NOT MATCHED AND nf.open_to_public = 'y' THEN INSERT
      (id, name, datum, zone, northing, easting,
       lat_lon, county_id, open_to_public,
       owner_id, description, confirmed_date)
      VALUES (nf.id, nf.name, nf.datum, nf.zone,
          nf.northing, nf.easting, nf.lat_lon,
          nf.county_id, nf.open_to_public,
          nf.owner_id, nf.description,
          nf.confirmed_date);
```

In DB2, a DELETE is something you can specify *in place of* an UPDATE. In Oracle, a DELETE can happen *after* an UPDATE.

Nulls

When writing SQL, it's critical to understand nulls and three-valued logic. With few exceptions, the result of any expression involving a null will be either null or unknown, and this has ramifications for any expression (comparison or otherwise) that you write.

Predicates for Nulls

You should not compare a null to any other value using the standard comparison operators. For example, the following query will *not* return all rows from the upfall table:

```
SELECT u.id, u.name, u.datum
FROM upfall u
WHERE u.datum = 'NAD1927'
    OR u.datum <> 'NAD1927';
```

You'd think that any given datum would either be NAD1927 or not be NAD1927, but this is not the case. A null datum is not NAD1927, nor is it not *not* NAD1927.

SQL provides the IS NULL and IS NOT NULL predicates to detect the presence or absence of null. To find all datum values other than NAD1927, including those that are null, specify:

```
SELECT u.id, u.name, u.datum
FROM upfall u
WHERE u.datum IS NULL
    OR u.datum <> 'NAD1927';
```

Similarly, you can use IS NOT NULL to match non-null values explicitly.

Using CASE with Nulls

CASE expressions can sometimes be helpful when working with potentially null data. For example, you can use CASE to ensure that you always get a non-null datum in your result set:

```
SELECT u.id, u.name,
    CASE WHEN u.datum IS NULL THEN
        '*None!*'
    ELSE u.datum END
FROM upfall u;
```

Most databases also provide functions to do this type of thing more succinctly.

Using the COALESCE Function

All platforms support the standard SQL COALESCE function. It takes a series of values and returns the first non-null value encountered. For example, to return a list of waterfall descriptions that show name when a description is null and show Unknown! when even the name is null, specify:

```
SELECT id, COALESCE(description, name, '*Unknown!*')
FROM upfall;
```

You can provide any number of arguments, but you should ensure that at least one will be non-null. If all arguments are null, COALESCE returns null as well.

Functions for Nulls: DB2

DB2 supports CASE and COALESCE. It also supports the NULLIF function, which returns null whenever the two input values are the same. Notice the effect of NULLIF in the first row of these results:

```
SELECT u.name, NULLIF(u.name,'Miners Falls')
FROM upfall u
WHERE u.name LIKE '%Miners%';

NAME                2
--------------- ---------------
Miners Falls
Little Miners    Little Miners
```

DB2 also now supports the same DECODE and NVL functions as Oracle does. See the section "Functions for Nulls: Oracle" on page 91.

Functions for Nulls: MySQL

MySQL supports CASE and COALESCE. In addition, it supports a function called IFNULL to return an alternate value for a potentially null input value. For example:

```
SELECT id, name, IFNULL(datum, '*None!*')
FROM upfall;
```

As with DB2, MySQL supports NULLIF to return null whenever two input values are the same:

```
SELECT u.name, NULLIF(u.name,'Miners Falls')
FROM upfall u
WHERE u.name LIKE '%Miners%';
```

You can also use the IF function to return one of two values, depending on whether an expression is TRUE:

```
SELECT id, name, IF(datum IS NULL,
                    '*None!*', datum)
FROM upfall;
```

You'd normally use a comparison expression to generate the Boolean TRUE/FALSE value for the first argument. If the expression evaluates to TRUE, the value from the second argument is returned. If the expression evaluates to FALSE or null, the third argument's value is returned.

Functions for Nulls: Oracle

Oracle supports CASE and COALESCE. It also provides several other functions for dealing with nulls.

NVL is similar to COALESCE. It is supported for backward compatibility and allows only two arguments:

```
SELECT id, name, NVL(datum, '*None!*')
FROM upfall;
```

NVL2 returns one of two values, depending on whether the first is null:

```
SELECT id, name, NVL2(datum, datum, '*None!*')
FROM upfall;
```

DECODE is equivalent to an inline IF statement (although you should really use CASE today), and it provides yet another way of dealing with nulls. The following example uses DECODE to replace *some* county_id values from upfall with their respective names:

```
SELECT id, name,
    DECODE(county_id,
           2, 'Alger County',
```

```
              6, 'Baraga County',
              NULL, 'Unknown',
              'Other')
   FROM upfall;
```

In this example, counties 2 and 6 translate to Alger and Baraga Counties, respectively. Any null county_id results in a value of 'Unknown'. Any other gov_unit_ids are denoted as 'Other'. DECODE supports any number of input/result pairs.

Functions for Nulls: PostgreSQL

PostgreSQL supports CASE and COALESCE. It also supports NULLIF as described in the section "Functions for Nulls: DB2" on page 90.

Functions for Nulls: SQL Server

SQL Server supports CASE, COALESCE, and an ISNULL function:

```
ISNULL(possible_null, alternative_value)
```

When *possible_null* is null, ISNULL will return *alternative_value*. Otherwise, ISNULL will return *possible_null*.

SQL Server 2008 supports the same NULLIF function that DB2 supports, returning NULL when both input values match.

SQL Server also supports a setting known as ANSI_NULLS, which affects the behavior of the = and <> predicates that compare to null:

```
... WHERE city_name = NULL
... WHERE city_name <> NULL
```

By default, neither of these predicates will ever match any rows. However, if you issue the command SET ANSI_NULLS OFF, you can use = NULL and <> NULL to search for NULL or NOT NULL values, respectively.

Numeric Conversions: DB2

Use the following functions to convert between different numeric types or between numeric and text types:

```
BIGINT(numeric)
BIGINT(character)
CHAR(integer)
CHAR(decimal [,decimal_character])
CHAR(floating [,decimal_character])
DECFLOAT(numeric, 16or34)
DECFLOAT(character, 16or34
        [, decimal_character])
DECIMAL(numeric [,precision[,scale]])
DECIMAL(character [,precision[,scale
                    [,decimal_character]]])
DOUBLE(numeric)
DOUBLE(character)
DOUBLE_PRECISION(numeric)
FLOAT(numeric)
REAL(numeric)
SMALLINT(numeric)
SMALLINT(character)
```

See "Datetime Conversions: DB2" on page 21 for information on converting between dates and numbers.

In the syntax, *numeric* can be any numeric type or expression; *character* can be any fixed- or variable-length character type or expression; *integer* can be any integer type or expression; and *decimal* can be any decimal type or expression.

NOTE

DB2 also provides compatibility with TO_CHAR and TO_NUMBER, as implemented by Oracle. See the section "Numeric Conversions: Oracle" on page 95 for details.

Each function converts its argument to the type indicated by the function name. The following example shows DECFLOAT being used to convert from a character string:

```
SELECT DECFLOAT('100.123451234512345',16)
FROM dual;
```

```
100.1234512345123
```

And following is an example showing CHAR and DECIMAL being used to convert back and forth between numbers and strings:

```
SELECT CHAR(100.12345),
       CHAR(DECIMAL('100.12345',5,2))
FROM pivot WHERE x=1;
```

```
100.12345   100.12
```

DECIMAL's default scale is zero when converting from a character string. To preserve digits to the right of the decimal point in that situation, you must specify a scale, which forces you to first specify a precision. No rounding occurs. To round a value being converted, you must first specify a precision and scale sufficient to hold the raw value, and then apply the ROUND function:

```
SELECT DECIMAL('10.999',4,2),
       DECIMAL('10.999',4),
       ROUND(DECIMAL('10.999',5,3),2)
FROM pivot WHERE x=1;
```

```
10.99     10.    11.000
```

You can use the optional *decimal_character* parameter to specify the character to use for the decimal point:

```
SELECT DECFLOAT('10/95',16,'/'), CHAR(10.95,'/')
FROM pivot WHERE x=1;
```

```
10.95 10/95
```

When converting to an integer type, any decimal portion is truncated.

Numeric Conversions: MySQL

MySQL implements the following numeric conversion functions:

FORMAT(*number* , *scale*)
> Provides general-purpose numeric conversions to text. The *scale* is the number of decimal places that you wish to appear in the result.

CONV(*number* , *from_base* , *to_base*)
> Converts from one base to another. The *number* may be either an integer or a string, and the base may range from 2 through 36.

BIN(*number*)
> Returns the binary representation of a base-10 *number*.

OCT(*number*)
> Returns the octal representation of a base-10 *number*.

HEX(*number*)
> Returns the hexadecimal representation of a base-10 *number*.

For example:

```
SELECT CONV('AF',16,10), HEX(175), FORMAT(123456.789,2);

175    AF    123,456.79
```

Use CAST to convert a string to a number.

Numeric Conversions: Oracle

Use the following functions in Oracle to convert to and from the supported numeric types:

```
TO_NUMBER(string, format)
TO_BINARY_DOUBLE(string, format)
TO_BINARY_FLOAT(string, format)
TO_CHAR(number, format)
TO_BINARY_DOUBLE(number)
TO_BINARY_FLOAT(number)
TO_NUMBER(number)
```

Use TO_NUMBER and TO_CHAR (the only two functions available prior to Oracle Database 10g) to convert between NUMBER and VARCHAR2 (Table 9 lists the available numeric format elements):

```
SELECT
    TO_CHAR(1234.56,'C9G999D99') to_char,
    TO_NUMBER('1,234.56','9G999D99') from_char,
    TO_CHAR(123,'999V99') v_example
FROM dual;

TO_CHAR           FROM_CHAR              V_EXAMPLE
----------------  ---------------------  ---------
     USD1,234.56  1234.56                    12300
```

Use TO_BINARY_FLOAT and TO_BINARY_DOUBLE to convert to the new 32- and 64-bit IEEE 754 floating-point types added in Oracle Database 10g. Also use these functions to convert values from one numeric type to another.

Table 9. Oracle's numeric format elements

Element	Description
$	Prefix: dollar sign ($).
, (comma)	Location of comma. Consider G instead.
. (period)	Location of period. Consider D instead.
0	Significant digit. Leading zeros.
9	Significant digit. Leading blanks.
B	Prefix: returns zero as blanks.
C	Location of ISO currency symbol.
D	Location of decimal point.
EEEE	Suffix: use scientific notation.
FM	Prefix: removes leading/trailing blanks.
G	Location of group separator.
L	Location of local currency symbol.
MI	Suffix: trailing minus (–) sign.
PR	Suffix: angle brackets (< and >) around negative values.
RN or rn	Roman numerals, upper- or lowercase. Output-only.

Element	Description
S	Prefix: leading plus (+) or minus (−) sign.
TM, TM9, TME	Prefix: use minimum number of characters (text-minimum). Output-only. TM9 gives decimal notation. TME gives scientific notation.
U	Specifies location of Euro symbol (€).
V	Multiplies the number to the left of the V in the format model by 10 raised to the *n*th power, where *n* is the number of 9s found after the V in the format model. See the example earlier in this section. Output-only.
X	Use hexadecimal notation. Output-only. Precede with 0s for leading zeros. Precede with FM to trim leading/trailing spaces.

Numeric Conversions: PostgreSQL

You can convert between numeric values and their string representations using the following functions, where *number* can be any numeric type:

```
TO_CHAR(number, format)
TO_NUMBER(string, format)
```

PostgreSQL's number format elements closely follow Oracle's. They are listed in Table 10.

Table 10. PostgreSQL's numeric format elements

Element	Description
$	Prefix: dollar sign ($).
, (comma)	Location of comma. Consider G instead.
. (period)	Location of period. Consider D instead.
0	Significant digit. Leading zeros.
9	Significant digit. Leading blanks.
B	Prefix: returns zero as blanks.
C	Location of ISO currency symbol.
D	Location of decimal point.
EEEE	Suffix: use scientific notation.

Element	Description
FM	Prefix: removes leading/trailing blanks.
G	Location of group separator.
L	Location of local currency symbol.
MI	Suffix: trailing minus (−) sign.
PR	Suffix: angle brackets (< and >) around negative values.
RN or rn	Roman numerals, upper- or lowercase. Output-only.
S	Prefix: leading plus (+) or minus (−) sign.
TM, TM9, TME	Prefix: use minimum number of characters (text-minimum). Output-only. TM9 gives decimal notation. TME gives scientific notation.
U	Specifies location of Euro symbol (€).
V	Multiplies the number to the left of the V in the format model by 10 raised to the nth power, where n is the number of 9s found after the V in the format model. See the example in "Numeric Conversions: Oracle" on page 95. Output-only.
X	Use hexadecimal notation. Output-only. Precede with 0s for leading zeros. Precede with FM to trim leading/trailing spaces.

Numeric Conversions: SQL Server

Use the CONVERT function for conversions to and from numeric values:

```
CONVERT(datatype[(length)], expression[, style])
```

Table 11 lists styles for converting FLOAT and REAL values to character strings. Table 12 lists styles for converting MONEY and SMALLMONEY values to character strings.

Table 11. SQL Server floating-point styles

Style	Description
0	Default, 0–6 digits, scientific notation when necessary
1	Eight digits + scientific notation
2	16 digits + scientific notation

Table 12. SQL Server money styles

Style	Description
0	Money default, no commas, two decimal digits
1	Commas every three digits, two decimal digits
2	No commas, four decimal digits

The following two examples demonstrate numeric conversions using the CONVERT function. The second example combines conversion from text with a monetary conversion:

```
SELECT CONVERT(VARCHAR(10), 1.234567, 2);

1.234567

SELECT CONVERT(
           VARCHAR,
               CONVERT(MONEY, '20999.95'), 1);

20,999.95
```

Numeric/Math Functions

Following are some useful numeric and math functions that are fairly universal across database platforms:

ABS(*number*)
> Returns the absolute value of *number*.

CEIL(*number*) or CEILING(*number*)
> Returns the smallest integer that is greater than or equal to the number that you pass. Use CEILING for SQL Server and CEIL for other platforms. Remember that with negative numbers, the *greater* value has the lower *absolute* value: CEIL(5.5) is 6, whereas CEIL(-5.5) is -5.

EXP(*number*)
> Returns the mathematical constant e (≈ 2.71828183)— also known as *Euler's constant*—raised to the power of *number*.

FLOOR(*number*)

Returns the largest integer that is less than or equal to the number you pass. Remember that with negative numbers, the *lesser* value has the higher *absolute* value: FLOOR(5.5) is 5, whereas FLOOR(-5.5) is -6.

LN(*number*)

Returns the natural logarithm of *number*. Supported in DB2, Oracle, and PostgreSQL. For other platforms, use LOG instead.

LOG(*number*)

Returns the natural logarithm of *number* (in DB2, SQL Server, and MySQL). In PostgreSQL, it returns the base-10 logarithm of *number*.

LOG(*base* , *number*)

Returns the logarithm of *number* in a *base* that you specify (Oracle and PostgreSQL).

LOG10(*number*)

Returns the base-10 logarithm of *number* (DB2, MySQL, and SQL Server).

MOD(*top* , *bottom*)

Returns the remainder of *top* divided by *bottom* (DB2, MySQL, Oracle, and PostgreSQL).

NANVL(*value* , *alternate*)

Returns an alternate value for any floating-point NaN (Not-a-Number) *value*. If *value* is NaN, then *alternate* is returned; otherwise, *value* is returned (Oracle).

REMAINDER(*top* , *bottom*)

Returns the remainder of *top* divided by *bottom*, the same as MOD (Oracle).

ROUND(*number* [, *places*])

Rounds *number* to a specified number of decimal *places*. The default is to round to an integer value. Use a negative value for *places* to round to the *left* of the decimal point. SQL Server requires the *places* argument.

ROUND(*number*, *places* [, *option*])
> SQL Server's version of ROUND. Use *option* to specify whether rounding or truncating is performed (see TRUNC below). If *option* is 0, the function rounds; otherwise, the function truncates.

SIGN(*number*)
> Indicates the sign of a number. SIGN returns –1, 0, or 1, depending on whether *number* is negative, zero, or positive.

TRUNC(*number* [, *precision*])
> Truncates *number* to a specific number of decimal places. The default *precision* is zero decimal places. Use a negative *precision* to truncate to the left of the decimal point, forcing those digits to zero. SQL Server implements truncation using a special form of ROUND. MySQL implements truncation using TRUNCATE(*number*, *precision*), requiring that you specify *precision*.

OLAP Functions

Online analytical processing (OLAP) function is the term DB2 uses for what the SQL standard refers to as a *window function*. See "Window Functions" on page 172 for more on this extremely useful class of functions.

Pivoting and Unpivoting

Oracle Database (11g Release 1 onward) and SQL Server (2005 onward) both support pivot and unpivot operators. With the PIVOT operation, you can present data in a grid format by turning rows into columns while aggregating some value of interest. The UNPIVOT operation turns columns into rows, allowing you to take multiple columns containing the same type of data and present that data as one column for reporting or analysis.

Pivoting: The Concept

Use the pivot operation to create a lookup table presenting values termed *measures* at the intersection of other values, termed *dimensions*. For example, say that you wish to report on the number of falls open or closed to the public by county. You might begin with the following query:

```
SELECT county_id,
       COALESCE(open_to_public, 'n')
          AS open_to_public,
       COUNT(id)
FROM upfall
GROUP BY county_id, open_to_public;
```

And you would get row-by-row results like these:

```
COUNTY_ID O  COUNT(ID)
---------- - ----------
***          n         1
        11 y         1
         2 y        11
         6 y         1
         7 y         2
        10 y         1
         9 y         1
```

Looking carefully at the output, you can see that county #7 has two falls open to the public. The information is all there, but the presentation is cumbersome and not at all compact.

A more useful presentation might be the following grid, which allows you to scan down to find the county, and then over to find the number of open and closed falls within that county:

```
COUNTY_ID       Open     Closed
----------  ----------  ----------
***                 0         1
         6          1         0
        11          1         0
         2         11         0
         7          2         0
         9          1         0
        10          1         0
```

You can use the PIVOT operator in both Oracle and SQL Server to generate these results.

Pivoting: Oracle

You can use the following query to generate results in the tabular format at the end of the preceding section. Essentially, the query converts the open/closed counts for each county from two rows into two columns:

```
SELECT *
FROM
    (SELECT id,
            county_id,
            COALESCE(open_to_public, 'n')
                AS open_to_public
     FROM upfall)
PIVOT (
    COUNT(id)
    FOR open_to_public IN (
        'y' AS "Open",
        'n' AS "Closed"
    )
);
```

Here's how the query works:

1. The subquery in the FROM clause generates the three values used to create the grid: the county ID for the vertical dimension; the open/closed flag for the horizontal dimension; and the waterfall ID to use as the measure by which to generate values for each combination of vertical and horizontal dimensions.

2. The COALESCE function call in the subquery ensures that the open_to_public flag is never null. (You may or may not need or want such behavior in your own queries.)

3. The query generates one row per county, because county_id is the only column not listed in the PIVOT clause.

4. The query generates one column for each listed value of open_to_public. Each column is given the name specified in the FOR clause: either Open or Closed in this case.

5. All the intersecting points in the grid are filled in by executing the expression COUNT(id) for each combination of county_id and open_to_public values.

Oracle further allows you to pivot on multiple columns. Following is an example query that presents the very same information, but this time as one long row:

```
SELECT *
FROM
    (SELECT id,
            county_id,
            COALESCE(open_to_public, 'n')
                AS open_to_public
     FROM upfall)
PIVOT (
    COUNT(id)
    FOR (county_id, open_to_public) IN (
        (2, 'y') AS "Alger Open",
        (2, 'n') AS "Alger Closed",
        (6, 'y') AS "Baraga Open",
        (6, 'n') AS "Baraga Closed",
        (7, 'y') AS "Ontonagon Open",
        (7, 'n') AS "Ontonagon Closed",
        (9, 'y') AS "Dickinson Open",
        (9, 'n') AS "Dickinson Closed",
        (10, 'y') AS "Gogebic Open",
        (10, 'n') AS "Gogebic Closed",
        (11, 'y') AS "Delta Open",
        (11, 'n') AS "Delta Closed",
        (NULL, 'y') AS "Unknown Open",
        (NULL, 'n') AS "Unknown Closed"
    )
);
```

Notice that the FOR clause specifies two column names. Further notice that each entry in the IN list specifies a combination of those same two values. The result will be the following single row:

```
Alger Open Alger Closed Baraga Open ...
---------- ------------ -----------
        11            0           1
```

The reason this second query returns only a single row is that the PIVOT clause consumes *all* of the columns returned by the subquery. Thus, no column(s) remain to serve as a vertical dimension. The result is a table having only a horizontal dimension and having one measure for each dimension value.

Pivoting: SQL Server

SQL Server supports a pivot operator as well, though with a different syntax from Oracle's implementation. Following is the query to generate the same tabular format as shown at the end of "Pivoting: The Concept" on page 102:

```
SELECT county_id,
       [1] as 'open',
       [0] as 'closed'
FROM
    (SELECT
        id,
        county_id,
        CASE open_to_public
           WHEN 'y' THEN 1
           ELSE 0 END AS open_to_public
     FROM upfall) AS SourceTable
PIVOT (
    COUNT(id)
    FOR open_to_public IN ([1], [0])
) AS PivotTable
```

Here's how this query operates:

1. The subquery in the FROM clause generates the three values to create the grid. You are required to specify an alias, which in this case is done using the AS clause.

2. The CASE statement in the subquery translates the y and n values into numeric ones and zeros. This is because SQL Server is currently unable to pivot on character columns.

3. The outer query lists county_id as the first column, because that column is the unpivoted column. One row is

ultimately returned for each unpivoted value: in this case for each `county_id`.

4. The second and third columns listed in the outer SELECT specify the column headings to use for the pivoted data.

5. The FOR...IN clause specifies that the first column is a count of open waterfalls (1=open to public) and that the second column is a count of closed waterfalls.

6. The `COUNT(id)` expression generates the summary values—in this case a count—for each of the cells.

7. All the intersecting points in the grid are filled in by executing the expression `COUNT(id)` for each combination of `county_id` and `open_to_public` values.

Unlike Oracle, SQL Server does not currently allow pivoting on two columns.

Unpivoting: The Concept

Sometimes you'll find yourself working with a table having two or more columns containing the same type of information. For example, you might have two or more phone numbers per row. Or, as in our case, you might choose to treat northing and easting values as two occurrences of a distance, which in fact they are.

Following is a simple query to show the northing and easting values as they are represented in the database table:

```
SELECT id, northing, easting
FROM upfall
WHERE northing IS NOT NULL
  OR easting IS NOT NULL;
```

The output presents northing and easting each in its own column:

```
        ID   NORTHING    EASTING
---------- ---------- ----------
         1    5141184     528971
         2    5140000     528808
         3    5137795     527046
```

And here is the same data presented with the distance values all in one column:

```
        ID LABEL       VALUE
---------- -------- ----------
         1 NORTHING    5141184
         1 EASTING      528971
         2 NORTHING    5140000
         2 EASTING      528808
         3 NORTHING    5137795
...
```

This second presentation is the unpivoted form.

Unpivoting: Oracle

You can generate the unpivoted form shown at the end of the preceding section using the following query:

```
SELECT id, label, value
FROM upfall
UNPIVOT EXCLUDE NULLS (
    value
    FOR label IN (northing, easting)
);
```

Here is an explanation of the query. It begins from the inside and works outward.

1. The FOR clause specifies that values from the **northing** and **easting** columns are to be unpivoted by being turned into rows.

2. The identifier **label** (following FOR) specifies the name of a new column that Oracle Database creates to identify each unpivoted value in the query results. The SELECT clause lists this column, which receives the name of the original column containing each unpivoted value.

3. The identifier **value** specified following the first parenthesis in the UNPIVOT clause specifies the name for the new column created to hold the unpivoted values. The SELECT clause lists this column.

4. The EXCLUDE NULLS clause throws out any nulls that would otherwise appear in the `value` column. That is the default behavior. Specify INCLUDE NULLS to retain such null values.

5. The SELECT clause lists the `id` column, causing the query to return one combination of `label` and `value` for each waterfall (i.e., for each distinct `id` value).

Unpivoting: SQL Server

Following is the SQL Server UNPIVOT syntax to generate the results shown at the end of the section "Unpivoting: The Concept" on page 106:

```
SELECT id, label, value
FROM upfall
UNPIVOT (
    value
    FOR label IN (northing, easting)
) UnpivotTable
```

Notice the alias name `UnpivotTable` at the end of the subquery. SQL Server requires an alias for such a subquery.

Here is the step-by-step explanation of this unpivot query:

1. The FOR clause specifies that values from the `northing` and `easting` columns are to be unpivoted by being turned into rows.

2. The identifier `label` (following FOR) specifies the name of a new column to identify each unpivoted value in the query results. The SELECT clause lists this column, which receives the name of the original column containing each unpivoted value.

3. The identifier `value` following the first parenthesis in the UNPIVOT clause specifies the name for the new column created to hold the unpivoted values. The SELECT clause lists this column.

4. SQL Server throws out any nulls that would otherwise appear in the `value` column.

5. The SELECT clause lists the `id` column, causing the query to return one combination of label and value for each waterfall (i.e., for each distinct `id` value).

Predicates

Predicates are conditions you write in the WHERE, ON, and HAVING clauses of an SQL statement that determine which rows are affected, or returned, by that statement. For example, use the predicate `name = 'Wagner Falls'` to return data for only that particular waterfall:

```
SELECT u.zone, u.northing, u.easting
FROM upfall u
WHERE name = 'Wagner Falls';
```

Table 13 lists the available comparison operators. Some operators, such as IN and EXISTS, are more fully described in later subsections. Regular-expression operators are described under "Regular Expressions" on page 113. Operators for dealing with nulls are described under "Nulls" on page 88.

Table 13. Comparison operators

Operator	Description
!=, <>	Tests for inequality
<	Tests for less than
<=	Tests for less than or equal to
<=>	Null-safe test for equality; supported only by MySQL
=	Tests for equality
>	Tests for greater than
>=	Tests for greater than or equal to
BETWEEN	Tests whether a value lies within a given range
EXISTS	Tests whether rows exist matching conditions that you specify
IN	Tests whether a value is contained in a set of values that you specify or that are returned by a subquery
IS [NOT] NULL	Tests for nullity

Operator	Description
LIKE	Tests whether a value matches a pattern
REGEXP, RLIKE	Regular-expression comparison operator; supported only by MySQL
REGEXP_LIKE	Tests whether a value matches the pattern described by a regular expression; supported only by Oracle

EXISTS Predicates

Use EXISTS and NOT EXISTS to test for the existence of rows matching a set of conditions that you specify. For example, to return a list of all owners associated with at least one waterfall, specify:

```
SELECT o.id, o.name
FROM owner o
WHERE EXISTS (SELECT * FROM upfall u
              WHERE u.owner_id = o.id);
```

Replace EXISTS with NOT EXISTS to find all owners who are not associated with *any* waterfall.

Subqueries used in EXISTS predicates should usually be *correlated*, which means that a subquery's WHERE clause compares a column from the subquery with a column from the outer query.

IN Predicates

Use IN to test whether a value falls within a set of values. You can enumerate that set as a list of literal values, or you can return the set as the result of a subquery. The following example specifies a set of literal values:

```
SELECT o.id, o.name
FROM owner o
WHERE o.id IN (1,2,3,4);
```

This next example uses a subquery and restates the EXISTS query from the preceding section, which returns a list of owners associated with at least one waterfall:

```
SELECT o.id, o.name
FROM owner o
WHERE o.id IN (SELECT u.owner_id
                  FROM upfall u);
```

Watch out for nulls! If the subquery you use with a NOT IN predicate returns a null value for even one row in the set, the result of the NOT IN operation will never be true. Rather, it will always be unknown, and your query won't function as you expect.

BETWEEN Predicates

Use BETWEEN to see whether a value falls in a given range. For example:

```
SELECT c.name
FROM county c
WHERE c.population BETWEEN 5000 AND 10000;
```

Any BETWEEN predicate can easily be expressed using the >= and <= operators:

```
SELECT c.name
FROM county c
WHERE c.population >= 5000
   AND c.population <= 10000;
```

When writing BETWEEN predicates, always list the smallest value first.

LIKE Predicates

The LIKE and NOT LIKE predicates give you rudimentary pattern-matching capabilities. You can use the percent (%) and underscore (_) characters to match any number of characters or any one character, respectively. For example, to find all waterfalls containing the word "Miners" in their names, specify:

```
SELECT u.id, u.name
FROM upfall u
WHERE u.name LIKE '%Miners%';
```

Use NOT LIKE to find all falls without "Miners" in their names.

MySQL and PostgreSQL recognize the backslash (\) as an escape character by default. Use the escape character to specify pattern-matching characters literally. For example, to find all falls without a percent in their names:

```
SELECT u.id, u.name
FROM upfall u
WHERE u.name NOT LIKE '%\%%';
```

You can also use the ESCAPE clause to specify explicitly the escape character. The following example will run in DB2, Oracle, and SQL Server:

```
SELECT u.id, u.name
FROM upfall u
WHERE u.name NOT LIKE '%\%%' ESCAPE '\';
```

When specifying an escape character in MySQL or PostgreSQL, be aware that the backslash is also the string-literal escape character. Thus, to specify explicitly the backslash as the LIKE escape character, you must escape that backslash in the ESCAPE clause:

```
SELECT u.id, u.name
FROM upfall u
WHERE u.name NOT LIKE '%\%%' ESCAPE '\\';
```

Oracle also implements LIKEC, LIKE2, and LIKE4, which work with Unicode characters, code units, and code points, respectively.

Recursive Queries

See "Hierarchical Queries" on page 62. Also see "CONNECT BY Queries" on page 8 if you are using a release of Oracle Database prior to Oracle Database 11g Release 2.

Regular Expressions

MySQL, Oracle, PostgreSQL, and SQL Server support *regular expressions*. SQL Server and MySQL support them only for string comparison, whereas PostgreSQL adds support for a regular-expression substring function and Oracle provides support for that and much more.

Regular Expressions: MySQL

In MySQL, you can perform regular-expression pattern matching using the REGEXP predicate in a manner similar to LIKE:

```
string REGEXP pattern
```

REGEXP looks for the specified regular expression anywhere in the target string. For example, to search for variant spellings of Fumee Falls:

```
SELECT u.id, u.name
FROM upfall u
WHERE u.name REGEXP '(Fumee|Fumie|Fumy)';
```

MySQL's regular-expression pattern matching is case-insensitive for nonbinary strings. Because MySQL recognizes the backslash (\) as an escape character in string literals, you must use a double backslash (\\) to represent a single backslash in any pattern that you write as a literal.

Table 14 lists the regular-expression operators recognized by MySQL.

Table 14. MySQL regular-expression operators

Operator	Description
.	Matches any character, including newlines.
^	Matches beginning of string.
$	Matches end of string.
[. . .]	Matches any of a set of characters.
[^ . . .]	Matches any character *not* in a set.
[[.*xx*.]]	Matches a collation element.

Operator	Description
[: *class* :]	Specifies a character class within a bracket expression. For example, use [[:digit:]] to match all digits. Valid character classes are: [:alnum:], [:alpha:], [:blank:], [:cntrl:], [:digit:], [:graph:], [:lower:], [:print:], [:punct:], [:space:], [:upper:], [:xdigit:].
[= *chars* =]	Specifies an equivalence class.
[. *charname* .]	Use within a bracket expression to match a character by name. For example, use [[.tilde.]] or [~] to match the tilde (~). You'll find a list of character names in *regexp/cname.h*.
*	Matches zero or more.
+	Matches one or more.
?	Matches zero or one.
{ *x* }, { *x* , *y* }, { *x* ,}	Matches *x* times, from *x* to *y* times, or at least *x* times.
|	Delimits alternatives.
(. . .)	Defines a subexpression.
[[:<:]]	Matches the beginning of a word.
[[:>:]]	Matches the end of a word.

Regular Expressions: Oracle

Oracle Database 10*g* implements the following regular-expression functions:

```
REGEXP_COUNT(source_string, pattern
            [, position [, match_parameter]])

REGEXP_INSTR(source_string, pattern
            [, position [, occurrence
            [, return_option
            [, match_parameter
            [, subexpression]]]]])

REGEXP_LIKE (source_string, pattern
            [, match_parameter])
```

```
REGEXP_REPLACE(source_string, pattern
             [, replace_string
             [, position [, occurrence
             [, match_parameter]]]])

REGEXP_SUBSTR(source_string, pattern
            [, position [, occurrence
            [, match_parameter]]])
```

Parameters are as follows:

source_string

The string you wish to search.

pattern

A regular expression describing the text pattern you are searching for. This expression cannot exceed 512 bytes in length.

replace_string

The replacement text. Each occurrence of *pattern* in *source_string* is replaced by *replace_string*, which can use backreferences to refer to values that match subexpressions in the pattern.

position

The character position at which to begin the search. This defaults to 1 and must be positive.

occurrence

The occurrence of *pattern* you are interested in finding. This defaults to 1. Specify 2 if you want to find the second occurrence of the pattern, 3 for the third occurrence, and so forth.

return_option

Specify 0 (the default) to return the pattern's beginning character position. Specify 1 to return the ending character position.

match_parameter

A set of options, in the form of a character string, that changes the default manner in which regular-expression pattern matching is performed. You may specify any, all, or none of the following options, in any order:

'i'

Specifies case-insensitive matching.

'c'

Specifies case-sensitive matching.

'n'

Allows the period (.) to match the newline character. (Normally, that is not the case.)

'm'

Causes the caret (^) and dollar sign ($) to match the beginning and ending, respectively, of lines within the source string. Normally, the caret and dollar sign match only the very beginning and the very end of the source string, regardless of any newline characters within the string.

'x'

Ignores whitespace, preventing whitespace characters from matching themselves.

subexpression

Specify 0 to return the position at which the entire pattern matches (INSTR) or to return the substring matching the entire pattern (SUBSTR). Specify 1 through 9 to return the position corresponding to that subexpression of the pattern (INSTR) or to return the string corresponding to that subexpression (SUBSTR). Defaults to 0.

The NLS_SORT parameter setting determines whether case-sensitive or case-insensitive matching is done by default.

NOTE

For detailed information and examples of Oracle's regular-expression support, see the *Oracle Regular Expressions Pocket Reference* by Jonathan Gennick and Peter Linsley (O'Reilly).

Table 15 lists the regular-expression operators supported by these functions.

Table 15. Oracle regular-expression operators

Operator	Description
\	Escapes a metacharacter
\1 . . . \9	Backreferences an earlier subexpression; the *replace_string* parameter supports from \1 to \500
.	Matches any character
^	Matches beginning of line
$	Matches end of line
[. . .]	Matches any of a set of characters
[^ . . .]	Matches any character *not* in a set
[.xx.]	Encloses a collation element
[:*class*:]	Specifies a character class such as [:digit:], [:alpha:], or [:upper:] within a bracket expression
[=*chars*=]	Specifies an equivalence class
*	Matches zero or more
+	Matches one or more
?	Matches zero or one
{x}, {x,y}, {x,}	Matches x times, from x to y times, or at least x times
|	Delimits alternatives
(. . .)	Defines a subexpression

Table 16 lists additional Perl-influenced operators added in Oracle Database 10g Release 2.

Table 16. Perl-influenced regular-expression operators in Oracle

Operator	Description
\d	Matches any digit
\D	Matches any nondigit
\w	Matches a *word character*, which is defined to include alphabetic characters, numeric characters, and the underscore
\W	Matches any nonword character
\s	Matches any whitespace character
\S	Matches any nonwhitespace character
\A	Anchors an expression to the beginning of a string
\Z	Anchors an expression to the end of a string
*?	Nongreedy "zero or more" quantifier
+?	Nongreedy "one or more" quantifier
??	Nongreedy "zero or one" quantifier
{x}?, {x,y}?, {x,}?	Nongreedy versions of {x}, {x,y}, {x,}

Regular Expressions: PostgreSQL

PostgreSQL implements regular expressions in two ways. First, it provides support in the form of the SQL standard's SIMILAR TO predicate. For example, to find variant spellings of Fumee Falls, specify:

```
SELECT u.id, u.name
FROM upfall u
WHERE u.name SIMILAR TO '(Fumee|Fumie|Fumy) Falls';
```

Table 17 lists the regular-expression operators that you can use with SIMILAR TO. Use a backslash (\) to embed any of the operators as a literal character. Use the ESCAPE clause to specify an alternate escape character:

```
WHERE u.name
    SIMILAR TO '(Fumee|Fumie|Fumy) Falls'
    ESCAPE '@'
```

Table 17. PostgreSQL regular-expression operators

Operator	Description
_	Matches any single character
%	Matches any string of characters
(. . .)	Defines a subexpression
|	Denotes alternation
*	Matches zero or more
+	Matches one or more
?	Matches zero or one
{x}, {x,y}, {x,}	Matches x times, from x to y times, and at least x times
[. . .]	Matches any of a set of characters
[^ . . .]	Matches any character *not* in a set

The following form of the SUBSTRING function supports the operators in Table 17:

```
SUBSTRING(string FROM pattern FOR escape)
```

For example:

```
SELECT u.name
FROM upfall u
WHERE SUBSTRING(u.name
        FROM '(Fumee|Fumie|Fumy) Falls' FOR '\\')
      IS NOT NULL;
```

As with the other queries in this section, this query searches for alternate spellings of Fumee Falls.

Second, PostgreSQL implements Posix-style regular expressions. For example, to find waterfalls that are described by Michigan state highway names in the form M-28, M-1, and so forth, up to three digits, you can write:

```
SELECT u.name, u.description
FROM upfall u
WHERE u.description ~ '.*M-[[:digit:]]{1,3}';
```

The ~ operator returns TRUE when the text on the left matches the expression on the right. The match is case-sensitive. Use ~* for a case-insensitive match. Similarly, you can use !~ and !~* to return TRUE when the text to the left *does not* match the pattern.

The following two functions provide additional support for Posix-style regular expressions:

```
SUBSTRING(string FROM pattern)
REGEXP_REPLACE(source, pattern, replacement [,flags ])
```

For example, to change waterfall names from "Fumee Falls" to "Falls, Fumee," specify:

```
SELECT REGEXP_REPLACE(
    u.name, '(.+?) (Falls)', '\\2, \\1')
FROM upfall u;
```

The *flags* argument to REGEXP_REPLACE is optional. Specify **'i'** for a case-insensitive match, **'g'** to replace all matching substrings, or both (as in **'ig'** or **'gi'**). Flags must be lowercase.

Use backreferences \1 through \9 in the *replacement* string to insert subexpressions from the matched text (denoted by (. . .)). Use \& in the *replacement* string to insert the entire matched text. Use \\ to place a single backslash in the *replacement* string.

\1 through \9 are always backreferences. When multiple digits are involved, the construct is assumed to be a backreference if it is within the valid range of currently existing subexpressions. If the construct is outside the valid range, it is treated as an octal character escape. However, if the first digit is a zero, the construct is *always* treated as an octal character escape, regardless of where it falls in relation to the range.

Table 18 lists the Posix-style regular-expression operators available in PostgreSQL.

Table 18. PostgreSQL Posix-style regular-expression operators

Operator	Description
\	Escapes a metacharacter
\1 . . . \9 . . .	Backreferences an earlier subexpression
.	Matches any character
^	Matches beginning of line
$	Matches end of line
[. . .]	Matches any of a set of characters
[^ . . .]	Matches any character *not* in a set
[: *class* :]	Specifies a character class within a bracket expression; valid classes are: [:alnum:], [:alpha:], [:blank:], [:cntrl;], [:digit:], [:graph:], [:lower:], [:print:], [:punct:], [:space:], [:upper:], [:xdigit:]
[. *xx* .]	Encloses a collation element within a bracket expression
[= *chars* =]	Specifies an equivalence class within a bracket expression
[[:<:]]	Matches beginning of word
[[:>:]]	Matches ending of word
*	Matches zero or more
+	Matches one or more
?	Matches zero or one
{*x*}, {*x*,*y*}, {*x*,}	Matches *x* times, from *x* to *y* times, or at least *x* times
|	Delimits alternatives
(. . .)	Defines a subexpression
(?: . . .)	Defines a noncapturing subexpression
(?= . . .)	Anchors to the beginning of a subexpression match
(?! . . .)	Anchors to the point of a subexpression mismatch
\a	Matches the alert bell
\b	Matches backspace

Operator	Description
\B	Matches a backslash (\); synonym for \\
\cX	Matches a character in which the low-order five bits are the same as in the character X
\d	Matches any digit
\D	Matches any nondigit
\e	Matches the escape character
\f	Matches the form feed
\m	Anchors to the beginning of a word
\M	Anchors to the end of a word
\n	Matches newline
\r	Matches carriage return
\t	Matches horizontal tab
\uXXXX	Matches the UTF-16 codepoint specified by the four-digit hexadecimal number XXXX
\Uxxxxxxxx	Reserved for an eventual UTF-32 extension
\v	Matches vertical tab
\w	Matches a *word character*, which is defined to include alphabetic characters, numeric characters, and the underscore
\W	Matches any nonword character
\xHEX_DIGITS	Matches the character at code point HEX_DIGITS
\0	Matches the null character (hex 0)
\xx	Matches the character at octal code point xx when xx is not a backreference
\xxx	Same as \xx, but for three octal digits
\y	Anchors to either the beginning or ending of a word
\Y	Anchors to a point that is not the beginning or ending of a word
\s	Matches any whitespace character
\S	Matches any nonwhitespace character
\A	Anchors an expression to the beginning of a string
\Z	Anchors an expression to the end of a string

Operator	Description
*?	Nongreedy "zero or more" quantifier
+?	Nongreedy "one or more" quantifier
??	Nongreedy "zero or one" quantifier
{x}?, {x,y}?, {x,}?	Nongreedy versions of {x}, {x,y}, {x,}

Table 19 lists embedded regular-expression option letters that you can use to control overall matching behavior. To embed options in an expression, use the syntax (?xxx . . .), where each x is an option letter from the table. Specify as many xs as you need.

Table 19. PostgreSQL Posix-style option letters

Option	Description
a	Makes the rest of the expression a basic regular expression (BRE)
c	Specifies case-sensitive matching
e	Makes the rest of the expression an extended regular expression (ERE)
i	Specifies case-insensitive matching
m	Same as n
n	Specifies newline-sensitive matching
p	Specifies partial newline-sensitive matching
q	Makes the rest of the regular expression a literal (no more operators are recognized)
s	Specifies non-newline-sensitive matching (the default)
t	Specifies tight syntax
w	Specifies inverse partial newline-sensitive matching (a.k.a. *weird matching*)
x	Switches to expanded syntax

Regular Expressions: SQL Server

SQL Server supports a very limited regular-expression syntax for its version of the LIKE predicate. For example, to find Fumee Falls even if it is misspelled as "Fumie Falls," write:

```
SELECT *
FROM upfall
WHERE name LIKE 'Fum[ie]e Falls';
```

SQL Server does not support quantifiers, alternation, subexpressions, or backreferences. Table 20 lists the few operators that SQL Server does support.

Table 20. SQL Server regular-expression operators

Operator	Description
%	Matches any number of characters
_	Matches any character, including newlines
[. . .]	Matches any of a set of characters
[^ . . .]	Matches any character *not* in a set

Selecting Data

Use a SELECT statement, or *query*, to retrieve data from a database—typically from a table or view or from a combination of tables and views:

```
SELECT expression_list
FROM data_source
WHERE predicates
GROUP BY expression_list
HAVING predicates
ORDER BY expression_list
```

DB2, Oracle, PostgreSQL, and SQL Server support factoring out subqueries using a WITH clause. See "Hierarchical Queries" on page 62 and "Subqueries" on page 139 for some examples of this technique.

The SELECT Clause

Each expression in the SELECT clause becomes a column in the result set returned by the query. Expressions may be simple column names, may generate a new value using a column value as input, or may have nothing to do with any columns at all.

Listing the columns to retrieve

The SELECT clause specifies the individual data elements you want the statement to return. The simple case is to specify a comma-delimited list of one or more column names from the tables listed in the FROM clause:

```
SELECT id, name
FROM owner;
```

The result set for this query will contain the following columns:

```
ID          NAME
----------- ---------------
1           Pictured Rocks
2           Michigan Nature
3           AF LLC
4           MI DNR
5           Horseshoe Falls
```

Taking shortcuts with the asterisk

To return all columns from a table, you can specify a single asterisk rather than write out each column name:

```
SELECT *
FROM owner;
```

```
ID          NAME            PHONE         TYPE
----------- --------------- ------------- -------
1           Pictured Rocks  906.387.2607  public
2           Michigan Nature 517.655.5655  private
3           AF LLC                        private
4           MI DNR          906-228-6561  public
5           Horseshoe Falls 906.387.2635  private
```

The asterisk is a helpful shortcut when executing queries interactively because it can save you a fair bit of typing. However, it's a risky proposition to use the asterisk in program code because the columns in a table may change over time, causing your program to fail when more or fewer columns than expected are returned.

Writing expressions

You can use column names in expressions. The following statement predicts the effect of a 10 percent drop in population (rounded to zero decimal places):

```
SELECT name, ROUND(population * 0.90, 0)
FROM county;
```

It is not necessary for an expression in a SELECT list to refer to any column at all in the table or view from which you are selecting. In Oracle, it's very common to issue queries against a special table known as dual, as in the following query, which returns the current date and time:

```
SELECT SYSDATE
FROM dual;
```

In DB2, you can query sysibm.sysdummy1:

```
SELECT CURRENT_DATE
FROM sysibm.sysdummy1;
```

Your database system will evaluate such expressions for each row returned by the query. Oracle's dual table is special in that it holds only one row. Thus, the preceding query from dual will return only one value.

In SQL Server and MySQL, you can return the result of an expression without selecting from a table at all. For example, use the following to get the current time (SQL Server):

```
SELECT getdate();
```

A SELECT such as this one, in which no table is specified, is the SQL Server/MySQL equivalent of Oracle's SELECT...FROM dual.

Specifying result-set column names

SQL enables you to specify a name, or *alias*, for each expression in your SELECT list. To specify a column alias, place the alias name immediately after the column name or expression, separating the two by at least one space:

```
SELECT id, name,
       ROUND(population * 0.90, 0) est_pop
FROM county;
```

```
ID          NAME        EST_POP
----------  ----------  -------------------
2           Alger       8876
6           Baraga      7871
7           Ontonagon   7036
...
```

Alternatively, you can introduce a column alias using the AS keyword:

```
SELECT id, name,
       ROUND(population * 0.90, 0) AS est_pop
FROM county;
```

PostgreSQL 8.1 and earlier *require* the use of AS to introduce a column alias.

In a given situation, it may not be important to provide an alias for a simple column name such as id. However, it's very important to use aliases when working with expressions to give sensible names to the resulting columns.

Dealing with case and punctuation in names

By default, SQL is case-insensitive and converts keywords and identifiers (such as table and column names) to uppercase. In MySQL, case sensitivity depends on whether the underlying operating system is case-sensitive (with respect to filenames). Oddly, in PostgreSQL, the default is to convert to lowercase.

If you must specify an identifier in a case-sensitive manner, you can enclose it in double quotes. The following example uses double quotes to generate mixed-case column aliases. Note that the double quotes also allow for spaces to be included in the alias names:

```
SELECT id AS "Fall #", name AS "Fall Name"
FROM upfall;
```

```
Fall # Fall Name
------ ---------------
1      Munising Falls
2      Tannery Falls
3      Alger Falls
...
```

The ability to quote identifiers also enables you to work with column and table names containing mixed cases, spaces, and other unusual characters.

Using subqueries in a SELECT list

Current versions of all of the platforms allow you to embed a subquery in a SELECT list. Ensure that the embedded subquery is scalar: it must return zero or one rows and one column. When no row is returned, you get a null. You should also specify a column alias so that the corresponding result-set column has a simple name to which you can easily refer in your code. For example, the following query returns the number of waterfalls for each owner:

```
SELECT o.id, o.name,
       (SELECT COUNT(*) FROM upfall u
        WHERE u.owner_id = o.id) AS fall_count
FROM owner o;
```

Subqueries can be correlated or uncorrelated. The subquery in this example is correlated, meaning that it refers to the enclosing table.

Qualifying column names

You can qualify a column name by its table name. This is especially important when writing queries that involve multiple tables, because sometimes two tables will have columns with the same name. To qualify a column name, use dot notation, as in *table_name.column_name*. For example:

```
SELECT owner.id, owner.name
FROM owner;
```

If you qualify a column name by its table name, you can also qualify that table name by its schema or database name:

```
SELECT sqlpocket.owner.id
FROM sqlpocket.owner;
```

To make it easier to qualify column names, you can provide table aliases. The following example gives the alias o to the table owner:

```
SELECT o.id, o.name
FROM owner o;
```

or:

```
SELECT o.id
FROM sqlpocket.owner o;
```

Qualifying column names is often necessary to remove ambiguity in a query.

ALL and DISTINCT

Use the ALL and DISTINCT keywords to specify whether you want the SELECT operation to eliminate duplicate rows from the result set. Duplicate elimination typically involves a partial sorting of the data, though other approaches are possible and the approach taken depends upon the implementation.

Following are two examples showing the difference between ALL and DISTINCT:

```
SELECT ALL o.type, u.open_to_public
FROM owner o
JOIN upfall u ON o.id = u.owner_id;

TYPE     OPEN_TO_PUBLIC
-------  --------------
public   y
private  y
private  y
public   y
public   y
public   y
```

```
SELECT DISTINCT o.type, u.open_to_public
FROM owner o
JOIN upfall u ON o.id = u.owner_id;

TYPE      OPEN_TO_PUBLIC
-------   --------------
private   y
public    y
```

The first query simply returns one row for each owner. (The ALL keyword is optional and is assumed by default.) The second uses DISTINCT to return a list of different type/open_to_public combinations. Use DISTINCT when you need each combination of column values to be returned only one time.

The FROM Clause

Use the FROM clause to specify the source of the data you want to retrieve. The simplest case is to specify a single table or view in the FROM clause of a SELECT statement:

```
SELECT name
FROM upfall
WHERE id = 2;
```

You can also qualify a table or view name with either a schema or database name, depending on your platform. Use dot notation for that purpose:

```
SELECT name
FROM sqlpocket.upfall
WHERE id = 2;
```

This query retrieves specifically from the upfall table or view owned by the user sqlpocket.

Table aliases in the FROM clause

You can specify a name, or *table alias*, for any table or view expression in a FROM clause. Aliases are useful for queries having ambiguous column names resulting from a join or the use of a subquery. For example, the following query returns a list of waterfalls, and for each fall, it shows the number of other falls in the same county:

```
SELECT u.name,
       (SELECT COUNT(*) FROM upfall u2
        WHERE u2.county_id = u.county_id)
FROM upfall u;
```

You couldn't write this query without using aliases because the table names are identical. You also lose the ability to reference the outer query from the inner query. For example, without aliases, this query's WHERE clause would be:

```
WHERE county_id = county_id
```

Using aliases is the only way to differentiate between the two references to the `upfall` table.

Subqueries in the FROM clause

Subqueries can sometimes be used to good effect in the FROM clause, where they are also known as *inline views*. Such subqueries must be *noncorrelated*; in other words, they must not reference columns from the main query. For example, the following query lists all publicly owned falls:

```
SELECT u.name AS fall_name, o.name AS owner_name
FROM (SELECT * FROM owner
      WHERE type = 'public') o
JOIN upfall u ON o.id = u.owner_id;
```

The subquery conceptually materializes a temporary table of falls that are publicly owned. That temporary table is then joined to the `upfall` table.

Generating tables through the VALUES clause

DB2 and SQL Server 2008 allow the use of the VALUES clause to generate tables on the fly:

```
SELECT id, name
FROM (VALUES (1, 'Munising Falls'),
             (2, 'Tannery Falls'))
AS falls(id, name);
```

```
ID          NAME
----------- --------------
          1 Munising Falls
          2 Tannery Falls
```

Be sure to place parentheses around the entire VALUES clause and to separate value lists using commas.

The WHERE Clause

Use the WHERE clause to restrict query results to only those rows of interest. Rarely will you want all rows from a table. More often, you'll want rows that match specific criteria. The following example retrieves only those waterfalls located in Alger County that are publicly accessible:

```
SELECT u.name
FROM upfall u
WHERE
   u.open_to_public = 'y'
   AND u.county_id IN (
        SELECT c.id FROM county c
        WHERE c.name = 'Alger');
```

The query uses an equality predicate (=) to identify publicly accessible waterfalls and an IN predicate (IN) to identify falls in Alger County. See the section "Predicates" on page 109 for more examples and a list of predicates that you can use in the WHERE clause.

NOTE

Join conditions are also used to restrict data returned by a query. See "Joining Tables" on page 72.

The GROUP BY Clause

See the section "Grouping and Summarizing" on page 52.

The HAVING Clause

See the section "Grouping and Summarizing" on page 52.

The ORDER BY Clause

Use ORDER BY to specify how you want results to be sorted.
For example, the following returns a list of waterfalls sorted by
owner name, and then sorted within each owner by fall name:

```
SELECT COALESCE(o.name, 'Unknown') AS owner,
       u.name AS fall
FROM upfall u
LEFT OUTER JOIN owner o
   ON u.owner_id = o.id
ORDER BY o.name, u.name;
```

The default sort is an ascending sort. You can use the keywords
ASCENDING and DESCENDING (which you can abbreviate
ASC and DESC) to control the sort on each column. The following is a modification of the previous sort, but this time, it
sorts owner names in reverse order:

```
SELECT COALESCE(o.name, 'Unknown') AS owner,
       u.name AS fall
FROM upfall u
LEFT OUTER JOIN owner o
   ON u.owner_id = o.id
ORDER BY o.name DESC, u.name ASC;
```

You can sort by columns and expressions that are not in your
SELECT list:

```
ORDER BY o.id DESC, u.id
```

You can also sort by numeric column position:

```
SELECT COALESCE(o.name, 'Unknown') AS owner,
       u.name AS fall
...
ORDER BY 1 DESC, 2 ASC;
```

And, in Oracle, PostgreSQL, and SQL Server you can even sort by the results of a *correlated* subquery (i.e., one that references a column from the main query):

```
SELECT COALESCE(o.name, 'Unknown') AS owner,
       u.name AS fall
FROM upfall u
LEFT OUTER JOIN owner o
   ON u.owner_id = o.id
ORDER BY (SELECT COUNT(*) FROM upfall u2
            WHERE u2.owner_id = o.id) DESC,
            u.name;
```

The subquery returns the number of waterfalls owned by each owner, so the result of this query is to first list those falls whose owners own the greatest number of falls. A second sort is then performed on falls' names.

String Functions

The following sections show how to use functions to perform common string operations.

Searching a String

In DB2 and Oracle, use the following version of INSTR to find the location of a substring within a string:

```
INSTR(string, substring[, position[, occurrence]])
```

You can specify a starting *position* for the search, and you can request that a specific *occurrence* be found. If *position* is negative, the search begins from the end of the string.

NOTE

In Oracle Database 10g and higher, you can also use REGEXP_INSTR, as described in the section "Regular Expressions" on page 113.

Oracle implements INSTR, INSTRB, INSTR2, and INSTR4, which work in terms of the input character set, bytes, Unicode code units, and Unicode code points, respectively. DB2 implements INSTR (and also INSTRB in version 9.7).

DB2 also supports the LOCATE and POSSTR functions:

```
LOCATE(substring, string[, position])
POSSTR(substring, string)
```

Both functions return the first occurrence of *substring* within *string*. Zero is returned if no match is found. The default is to search *string* beginning from character position 1.

In SQL Server, use the CHARINDEX function:

```
CHARINDEX(substring, string[, position])
```

The arguments are the same as they are for DB2's LOCATE.

In MySQL, use either INSTR or LOCATE:

```
INSTR(string, substring)
LOCATE(substring, string[, position])
```

Use *position* to specify a starting character position other than 1. Zero is returned if *substring* is not found within *string*.

In PostgreSQL, use either POSITION or STRPOS:

```
POSITION(substring IN string)
STRPOS(string, substring)
```

Notice that the two functions use opposite argument orders.

Replacing Text in a String

Use the REPLACE function to perform a search-and-replace operation on a *string*:

```
REPLACE(string, search, replace)
```

You can delete occurrences of *search* by specifying an empty string (' ') as the *replace* text. Also, Oracle allows you to omit the replacement string, which has the same effect as specifying the empty string (' ').

Extracting a Substring

In DB2, Oracle, and PostgreSQL, you can use the SUBSTR function to extract *length* characters from a *string*, beginning at position *start*:

```
SUBSTR(string, start[, length])
```

Strings begin with position 1. Oracle treats a *start* of 0 as though you had specified 1. If *start* is negative, Oracle counts backward from the end of the *string*.

Omit *length* to get all characters from *start* to the end of the string. DB2 pads any result with spaces, if necessary, to ensure that the result is always *length* characters long.

Oracle implements SUBSTR, SUBSTRB, SUBSTR2, and SUBSTR4, which work in terms of the input character set, bytes, Unicode code units, and Unicode code points, respectively. DB2 implements SUBSTR (and also SUBSTRB in version 9.7). PostgreSQL implements only SUBSTR.

PostgreSQL also supports:

```
SUBSTRING(string FROM start)
SUBSTRING(string FROM start FOR length)
```

In SQL Server, use SUBSTRING. All three arguments are required:

```
SUBSTRING(string, start, length)
```

MySQL implements the following substring functions:

```
SUBSTRING(string, start)
SUBSTRING(string FROM start)
SUBSTRING(string, start, length)
SUBSTRING(string FROM start FOR length)
```

The arguments to these SUBSTRING functions are the same as they are for SUBSTR. MySQL supports a negative *start* position, which counts from the right.

Finding the Length of a String

Use the LENGTH function (LEN in SQL Server) to determine the length of a string:

```
LENGTH(string)
```

Oracle implements LENGTH, LENGTHB, LENGTH2, and LENGTH4, which count characters in the input character set, bytes, Unicode code units, and Unicode code points, respectively.

Concatenating Strings

The easiest way to concatenate strings is to use the SQL standard string concatenation operator (||):

```
string1 || string2
```

SQL Server does not support the ISO SQL string concatenation operator. Use a + instead:

```
string1 + string2
```

MySQL supports neither || nor + for concatenating strings, but it does support an unlimited number of string arguments to CONCAT:

```
CONCAT(string[, string ...])
```

PostgreSQL supports a TEXTCAT function:

```
TEXTCAT(string, string)
```

Trimming Unwanted Characters

LTRIM, RTRIM, and TRIM remove unwanted characters from a string. TRIM is part of the SQL standard; the others are not. TRIM's syntax is:

```
TRIM(string)
TRIM(character FROM string)
TRIM(option [character] FROM string)
option ::= {LEADING|TRAILING|BOTH}
```

Using TRIM, you can trim leading *characters*, trailing *characters*, or both from a string. The *character* to trim defaults to a single space. The default *option* is BOTH.

LTRIM removes *unwanted* characters from the beginning (left edge) of a *string*, whereas RTRIM removes from the end (right edge). The implementation for Oracle and PostgreSQL is:

```
LTRIM(string[, unwanted])
RTRIM(string[, unwanted])
```

The *unwanted* argument is a string containing the characters you want trimmed, and it defaults to a single space. For example, to remove various punctuation from both ends of a string, specify:

```
RTRIM(LTRIM(string,'.,! '),'.,! ')
```

DB2, MySQL, and SQL Server do not support the *unwanted* argument; you can trim only spaces.

Changing the Case of a String

Use the UPPER and LOWER functions to upper- or lowercase all letters in a string:

```
UPPER(string)
LOWER(string)
```

In DB2 9.7 and higher, Oracle, and PostgreSQL, you can also use INITCAP(*string*) to uppercase the first letter of each word in a string and lowercase the other letters. DB2 supports UCASE and LCASE as synonyms for UPPER and LOWER.

Subqueries

Subject to various platform restrictions, subqueries can be used in most SQL statements as follows:

In the SELECT list of a SELECT statement
    See "The SELECT Clause" on page 125.

In the FROM clause of a SELECT statement
    See "The FROM Clause" on page 130.

In the WHERE clause of a SELECT statement
    See "Predicates" on page 109, and also "The WHERE Clause" on page 132.

In the ORDER BY clause of a SELECT statement
    See "The ORDER BY Clause" on page 133.

In an INSERT…SELECT…FROM statement
    See "Subquery Inserts" on page 69.

In the SET clause of an UPDATE statement
    See "New Values from a Subquery" on page 169.

Subqueries in the FROM Clause

A subquery in the FROM clause of a SELECT statement functions like a view and replaces a table as a data source. You can use subqueries—just as you can use views—as targets of IN-SERT, DELETE, and UPDATE statements. For example, for all platforms except MySQL and SQL Server, you can specify:

```
DELETE
FROM (SELECT * FROM upfall u
      WHERE u.open_to_public = 'n') u2
WHERE u2.owner_id IS NOT NULL;
```

This statement deletes waterfalls that are not open to the public and for which an owner is known.

Subqueries in the WITH Clause

The SQL standard defines a WITH clause that you can use to
factor out a subquery so that you don't need to repeat it in your
SELECT statement. DB2, Oracle, PostgreSQL, and SQL Server
support WITH.

NOTE

See "Hierarchical Queries" on page 62 to learn how
WITH is used to write recursive queries.

The following SELECT repeats two subqueries twice to generate a list of counties containing more than the average
number of waterfalls per county:

```
SELECT c.name,
        (SELECT COUNT(*) FROM upfall u2
          WHERE u2.county_id = c.id) fall_count,
        (SELECT AVG(fall_count)
          FROM (SELECT COUNT(*) fall_count
                  FROM upfall u3
                  GROUP BY u3.county_id) x1) avg_count
FROM county c
WHERE (SELECT COUNT(*) FROM upfall u2
          WHERE u2.county_id = c.id)
      >
      (SELECT AVG(fall_count)
          FROM (SELECT COUNT(*) fall_count
                  FROM upfall u3
                  GROUP BY u3.county_id) x2);
```

Aside from being difficult to read and comprehend, this query
is a potential maintenance disaster because any change to
either subquery must be made twice. Using WITH, you can
rewrite the query in a way that specifies each subquery only
once. For example, in all but PostgreSQL:

```
WITH fall_count_query AS
        (SELECT u2.county_id id,
                COUNT(*) fall_count
          FROM upfall u2
          GROUP BY u2.county_id),
```

```
      avg_count_query AS
        (SELECT AVG(fall_count) avg_count
          FROM (SELECT COUNT(*) fall_count
                FROM upfall u3
                GROUP BY u3.county_id))
SELECT c.name,
       (SELECT fall_count FROM fall_count_query
        WHERE fall_count_query.id = c.id) fall_count,
       (SELECT avg_count FROM avg_count_query) avg_count
FROM county c
WHERE (SELECT fall_count FROM fall_count_query
       WHERE fall_count_query.id = c.id)
    > (SELECT avg_count FROM avg_count_query);
```

PostgreSQL requires an alias for any subquery in the FROM clause of a subquery in the WITH clause. For example, notice the alias fc at the end of the following snippet:

```
...
      avg_count_query AS
        (SELECT AVG(fall_count) avg_count
          FROM (SELECT COUNT(*) fall_count
                FROM upfall u3
                GROUP BY u3.county_id) fc)
...
```

The correlated subquery changes to a noncorrelated version as it moves into the WITH clause. The original query used the following subquery to retrieve the number of waterfalls for a given county:

```
(SELECT COUNT(*) FROM upfall u2
WHERE u2.county_id = c.id) fall_count,
```

In the WITH version of the query, the correlated subquery that counts waterfalls for a single county is replaced with a GROUP BY subquery that counts falls for *all* counties:

```
(SELECT u2.county_id id,
        COUNT(*) fall_count
FROM upfall u2
GROUP BY u2.county_id),
```

The "correlation" becomes a WHERE clause when selecting from the factored-out query:

```
(SELECT fall_count FROM fall_count_query
WHERE fall_count_query.id = c.id)
```

When moving a correlated subquery into the WITH clause, you'll need to uncorrelate it. Determining how best to accomplish this sometimes requires a bit of thought and experimentation.

Although the preceding query using the WITH clause is somewhat more complex than the one it replaces, the logic for computing the fall count and average fall count is now encapsulated in the WITH clause. The other subqueries do nothing more than select specific columns from the result sets of the WITH-clause queries. As the size of the subqueries increases, so does the apparent simplification.

Further refactoring is possible. This time, the `avg_count_query` references the previously defined `fall_count_query`, consolidating the logic for counting waterfalls by county into only one subquery:

```
WITH fall_count_query AS
        (SELECT u2.county_id id,
                COUNT(*) fall_count
         FROM upfall u2
         GROUP BY u2.county_id),
     avg_count_query AS
        (SELECT AVG(fall_count) avg_count
         FROM (SELECT * FROM fall_count_query))
SELECT c.name,
        (SELECT fall_count FROM fall_count_query
         WHERE fall_count_query.id = c.id) fall_count,
        (SELECT avg_count FROM avg_count_query) avg_count
FROM county c
WHERE (SELECT fall_count FROM fall_count_query
       WHERE fall_count_query.id = c.id)
    > (SELECT avg_count FROM avg_count_query);
```

DB2 and SQL Server support an alternative method for naming the result columns from a WITH-clause query. Instead of providing column names as aliases, you can provide them in parentheses following the query name:

```
WITH fall_count_query (id, fall_count) AS
```

The WITH clause doesn't eliminate multiple subqueries entirely. It does allow you to locate all of the complex logic in one place, leaving only simple SELECTs for the subqueries in the main statement.

Tables, Creating

You create a new table in a database by issuing a CREATE TABLE statement. The syntax varies widely among vendors, but the following subsections show reasonable examples for each platform. Bear in mind the following points:

- At a minimum, all you need is a list of column names and their data types:

  ```
  CREATE TABLE simple_example (
      id NUMERIC,
      name VARCHAR(15),
      last_changed DATE
  );
  ```

- The examples give explicit names for many of the constraints, which I consider a best practice, but the CONSTRAINT *constraint_name* syntax is optional and is often omitted (especially on column constraints such as the NOT NULL constraint).

- You can usually declare constraints that involve a single column as part of that column's definition. Multicolumn constraints must be declared as table-level elements. The examples demonstrate both approaches.

See the platform-specific sections on "Data Types" for lists of valid data types by platform.

Creating a Table: DB2

The following is a typical CREATE TABLE statement for DB2:

```
CREATE TABLE db2_example (
    id DECIMAL(6) NOT NULL
        GENERATED ALWAYS AS IDENTITY (
            START WITH 1 INCREMENT BY 1
            MAXVALUE 999999
            CACHE 20 NO ORDER),
```

```
        name VARCHAR(15) NOT NULL,
        country VARCHAR(2) DEFAULT 'CA' NOT NULL
            CONSTRAINT country_check
            CHECK (country IN ('CA','US')),
        indexed_name VARCHAR(15),
        CONSTRAINT db2_example_pk
            PRIMARY KEY (id),
        CONSTRAINT db2_example_fk01
            FOREIGN KEY (name, country)
            REFERENCES parent_example (name, country),
        CONSTRAINT db2_example_u01
            UNIQUE (name, country),
        CONSTRAINT db2_example_c01
            CHECK (indexed_name = UPPER(name))
    ) IN userspace1;
```

In DB2, you must specify NOT NULL explicitly for all primary key columns. Other vendors generally infer NOT NULL from your primary key specification. Likewise, DB2 requires NOT NULL on columns involved in UNIQUE constraints.

The `id` column in this table is automatically generated from a sequence of values from 1 to 9999999. Sequence values are cached in memory for faster access and are not necessarily assigned in order (which also improves performance).

Creating a Table: MySQL

The following is a typical CREATE TABLE statement for MySQL. The `id` column is autogenerated:

```
    CREATE TABLE mysql_example (
        id INTEGER AUTO_INCREMENT,
        name VARCHAR(15) NOT NULL,
        country VARCHAR(2) DEFAULT 'CA'
            NOT NULL
            CHECK (country IN ('CA','US')),
        indexed_name VARCHAR(15),
        CONSTRAINT mysql_example_pk
            PRIMARY KEY (id),
        CONSTRAINT mysql_example_fk01
            FOREIGN KEY (name, country)
            REFERENCES parent_example (name, country),
        CONSTRAINT mysql_example_u01
            UNIQUE (name, country),
```

```
      CONSTRAINT mysql_example_index_upper
         CHECK (indexed_name = UPPER(name))
   ) ENGINE = INNODB;
```

MySQL does not support the `CONSTRAINT` *constraint_name* syntax or the definition of foreign key and check constraints at the column level.

WARNING

MySQL silently ignores foreign key constraints, except between InnoDB tables. It will even silently ignore the declaration of such constraints to tables that do not exist, unless you are creating an InnoDB table.

MySQL supports different *storage engines*, which are physical mechanisms for storing table rows. Use the ENGINE keyword to specify an engine type. The following are valid engines in MySQL 5.1: ARCHIVE, BLACKHOLE, CSV, EXAMPLE, FEDERATED, INNODB, MEMORY, MERGE, MYISAM (called ISAM prior to 5.0), and NDBCLUSTER. MYISAM is the default, although that can be changed when starting the MySQL daemon.

NOTE

Earlier versions of MySQL require you to use the keyword TYPE rather than ENGINE.

Creating a Table: Oracle

The following is a typical CREATE TABLE statement for Oracle:

```
CREATE TABLE oracle_example (
   id NUMBER(6),
   name VARCHAR2(15) NOT NULL,
   country VARCHAR2(2) DEFAULT 'CA'
      CONSTRAINT country_not_null NOT NULL
      CONSTRAINT country_check
```

```
      CHECK (country IN ('CA','US')),
   indexed_name VARCHAR2(15),
   CONSTRAINT oracle_example_pk
      PRIMARY KEY (id),
   CONSTRAINT oracle_example_fk01
      FOREIGN KEY (name, country)
      REFERENCES parent_example (name, country),
   CONSTRAINT oracle_example_u01
      UNIQUE (name, country),
   CONSTRAINT oracle_example_index_upper
      CHECK (indexed_name = UPPER(name))
) TABLESPACE users;
```

This statement assigns the table to the **users** tablespace. The TABLESPACE clause is optional. If you aren't certain which tablespace to specify, you can either omit the clause to accept your default tablespace assignment or ask your database administrator's advice.

If you want the ID column to be an automatically generated sequential ID number, you can begin by creating an Oracle sequence:

```
CREATE SEQUENCE oracle_example_pk
   NOCYCLE MAXVALUE 999999 START WITH 1;
```

Then, create a trigger to derive a new **id** value from the sequence whenever a new row is inserted:

```
CREATE OR REPLACE TRIGGER oracle_example_pk
BEFORE INSERT ON oracle_example
FOR EACH ROW
DECLARE
   next_id NUMBER;
BEGIN
   SELECT oracle_example_pk.NEXTVAL INTO next_id
   FROM dual;

   :NEW.id := next_id;
END;
/
```

Oracle sequences generate values up to 10^{27}. Use the MAX-VALUE clause to constrain the value range to something that is appropriate to your application and does not exceed the range of your primary key column.

Creating a Table: PostgreSQL

The following is a typical CREATE TABLE statement for PostgreSQL:

```
CREATE TABLE postgre_example (
    id SERIAL,
    name VARCHAR(15) NOT NULL,
    country VARCHAR(2) DEFAULT 'CA'
        CONSTRAINT country_not_null NOT NULL
        CONSTRAINT country_check
        CHECK (country IN ('CA','US')),
    indexed_name VARCHAR(15),
    CONSTRAINT postgre_example_pk
        PRIMARY KEY (id),
    CONSTRAINT postgre_example_fk01
        FOREIGN KEY (name, country)
        REFERENCES parent_example (name, country),
    CONSTRAINT postgre_example_u01
        UNIQUE (name, country),
    CONSTRAINT postgre_example_index_upper
        CHECK (indexed_name = UPPER(name))
)TABLESPACE pg_default;
```

The **id** column's type is SERIAL, which results in an auto-incrementing four-byte integer. Support for tablespaces came about in PostgreSQL 8.0. The TABLESPACE clause is optional.

Creating a Table: SQL Server

The following is a typical CREATE TABLE statement for SQL Server, with an auto-incrementing primary key column that begins at 1 and increments by 1:

```
CREATE TABLE msss_example (
    id INT IDENTITY (1,1),
    name VARCHAR(15) NOT NULL,
    country VARCHAR(2) DEFAULT 'CA'
        CONSTRAINT country_not_null NOT NULL
        CONSTRAINT country_check
        CHECK (country IN ('CA','US')),
    indexed_name VARCHAR(15),
    CONSTRAINT msss_example_pk
        PRIMARY KEY (id),
```

```
CONSTRAINT msss_example_fk01
    FOREIGN KEY (name, country)
    REFERENCES parent_example (name, country),
CONSTRAINT msss_example_u01
    UNIQUE (name, country),
CONSTRAINT msss_example_index_upper
    CHECK (indexed_name = UPPER(name))
);
```

Tables, Dropping

When you no longer need a table, you can drop it from your schema:

```
DROP TABLE table_name;
```

In Oracle, you can drop a table that is referenced by foreign key constraints using the following syntax:

```
DROP TABLE table_name CASCADE CONSTRAINTS;
```

In PostgreSQL, you can do the same thing using:

```
DROP TABLE table_name CASCADE;
```

Foreign key constraints that reference the table being dropped will be dropped themselves.

NOTE

In DB2, referencing foreign key constraints are always dropped; no CASCADE clause is needed.

In all other cases, you must drop any referencing foreign key constraints manually before dropping the referenced table.

Tables, Modifying

You can change the columns and other attributes of a table using the ALTER TABLE statement. The syntax varies significantly among vendors. The following subsections show the same sequence of common table alterations. Many other types of changes are possible; consult your vendor documentation for details.

Modifying a Table: DB2

Use ALTER TABLE's ADD clause to add a column or table constraint. You may add more than one item at a time:

```
ALTER TABLE db2_example
    ADD COLUMN lower_name VARCHAR(15)
    ADD CONSTRAINT lower_name
        CHECK(lower_name = LOWER(name));
```

Use the ALTER clause to change a column's default value or data type. For example:

```
ALTER TABLE db2_example
    ALTER COLUMN name SET DEFAULT 'Missing!'
    ALTER COLUMN indexed_name
        SET DATA TYPE VARCHAR(30);
```

You can change only one item at a time for a given column. If you need to change both name *and* data type for a given column, you will need to issue separate ALTER TABLE statements for each of those two changes.

You can add table constraints but not column constraints, so the no_leading_space constraint added at the column level on other platforms must be added at the table level for DB2:

```
ALTER TABLE db2_example
    ADD CONSTRAINT no_leading_space
        CHECK (indexed_name = LTRIM(indexed_name));
```

DB2 9.7 and higher support changing the nullability of a column. For example:

```
ALTER TABLE db2_example
    ALTER COLUMN name SET NOT NULL;
```

To change the nullability of a column prior to DB2 9.7, you must drop and recreate the table. (Remember that columns participating in unique and primary key constraints cannot be nullable.) Unlike on the other platforms, there is no easy way to make name nullable. However, you can achieve the desired effect of adding NOT NULL to a column by creating a CHECK constraint:

```
ALTER TABLE db2_example
    ADD CONSTRAINT indexed_name_not
        CHECK (indexed_name IS NOT NULL);
```

To remove a constraint, use the DROP clause:

```
ALTER TABLE db2_example
    DROP CONSTRAINT lower_name
    DROP CONSTRAINT no_leading_space
    DROP CONSTRAINT indexed_name_not;
```

You cannot drop a column from a table in DB2. If avoiding the use of an unwanted column is not sufficient, you must drop and recreate the table.

Modifying a Table: MySQL

Use the ADD clause to add columns and constraints. Be sure to avoid using the same name for both a column and a constraint:

```
ALTER TABLE mysql_example
    ADD lower_name VARCHAR(15),
    ADD CONSTRAINT lower_name_chk
        CHECK (lower_name = LOWER(name));
```

To create new definitions for a column, use MODIFY. You must specify at least a data type for each column, and you may also specify a default value and nullability (e.g., NOT NULL). New definitions completely overwrite the old. Thus, in the following example, country will lose its existing default value because it was not respecified in the MODIFY clause:

```
ALTER TABLE mysql_example
    MODIFY name VARCHAR(30)
        DEFAULT 'Missing!' NULL,
    MODIFY country VARCHAR(2) NOT NULL,
    MODIFY indexed_name VARCHAR(30) NOT NULL;
```

Constraints—even those referencing a single column—must be added via the ADD clause:

```
ALTER TABLE mysql_example
    ADD CONSTRAINT no_leading_space
        CHECK (indexed_name = LTRIM(indexed_name));
```

MySQL does not allow you to drop CHECK constraints. You can drop primary key and foreign key constraints as follows:

```
ALTER TABLE table_name
    DROP PRIMARY KEY,
    DROP FOREIGN KEY constraint_name;
```

To drop a UNIQUE constraint, you must drop the index used to enforce it:

```
ALTER TABLE table_name
    DROP INDEX index_name;
```

Use DROP to remove a column:

```
ALTER TABLE mysql_example
    DROP COLUMN lower_name;
```

Modifying a Table: Oracle

Use ALTER TABLE...ADD to add columns and table constraints:

```
ALTER TABLE oracle_example ADD (
    lower_name VARCHAR2(15),
    CONSTRAINT lower_name
        CHECK (lower_name = LOWER(name))
);
```

Use MODIFY to change a column's data type, default value, or nullability. You can also add new constraints to a column. Anything you do not specify is left unchanged:

```
ALTER TABLE oracle_example MODIFY (
    name VARCHAR2(30) DEFAULT 'Missing!'
        CONSTRAINT name_canbe_null NULL,
    country DEFAULT NULL,
    indexed_name varchar2(30) NOT NULL
        CONSTRAINT no_leading_space
            CHECK (indexed_name = LTRIM(indexed_name))
);
```

Use DROP to remove a column or constraint. Each drop must be specified separately, and no parentheses are used:

```
ALTER TABLE oracle_example
    DROP CONSTRAINT lower_name;

ALTER TABLE oracle_example
    DROP COLUMN lower_name;
```

Modifying a Table: PostgreSQL

Use the ADD clause to add columns and constraints:

```
ALTER TABLE postgre_example
    ADD lower_name VARCHAR(15),
    ADD CONSTRAINT lower_name
        CHECK (lower_name = LOWER(name));
```

Use various ALTER clauses to change a column's data types, default values, and nullability:

```
ALTER TABLE postgre_example
    ALTER name TYPE VARCHAR(30),
    ALTER name SET DEFAULT 'Missing!',
    ALTER name DROP NOT NULL,
    ALTER country DROP DEFAULT,
    ALTER indexed_name TYPE VARCHAR(30),
    ALTER indexed_name SET NOT NULL;
```

Constraints—even those referencing a single column—must be added via the ADD clause:

```
ALTER TABLE postgre_example
    ADD CONSTRAINT no_leading_space
        CHECK (indexed_name = LTRIM(indexed_name));
```

Use DROP to remove a column or constraint:

```
ALTER TABLE postgre_example
    DROP CONSTRAINT lower_name,
    DROP COLUMN lower_name;
```

Modifying a Table: SQL Server

Use ALTER TABLE...ADD to add columns and table constraints:

```
ALTER TABLE msss_example ADD
    lower_name VARCHAR(15),
```

```
CONSTRAINT lower_name
    CHECK (lower_name = LOWER(name));
```

Issue ALTER TABLE...ALTER COLUMN to modify a column's data type or nullability. You can make only one alteration per statement:

```
ALTER TABLE msss_example
    ALTER COLUMN name
        VARCHAR(15) NULL;

ALTER TABLE msss_example
    ALTER COLUMN country
        VARCHAR(2) NULL;

ALTER TABLE msss_example
    ALTER COLUMN indexed_name
        VARCHAR(30) NOT NULL;
```

Column name's data type cannot be changed in this example because SQL Server does not allow data type changes for columns involved in certain types of constraints (e.g., foreign key constraints).

You cannot add column-level constraints—only table-level constraints. The following example adds a constraint that tests the value in a column, but the constraint is associated with the table, not with the column in question:

```
ALTER TABLE msss_example
    ADD CONSTRAINT no_leading_space
        CHECK (indexed_name = LTRIM(indexed_name));
```

Add or remove default values by adding or removing so-called *default constraints*. For example:

```
ALTER TABLE msss_example
    ADD CONSTRAINT name_default
        DEFAULT 'Missing!' FOR name;

ALTER TABLE msss_example
    DROP CONSTRAINT name_default;
```

To remove the default value from the country column, you must first look up the automatically generated constraint name (e.g., via the GUI), and then drop that constraint by specifying its name.

Use ALTER TABLE...DROP to remove a column or constraint:

```
ALTER TABLE msss_example
   DROP CONSTRAINT no_leading_space;
```

Transaction Management

A *transaction* is a collection of operations treated as a unit. Either all operations in the unit are completed or none of them are. All commonly used databases make provisions for transactions.

When working in a transactional environment, you need to know how to begin and end a transaction. You also need to know how to specify various characteristics of a transaction—for example, whether it will update any data.

Autocommit Mode

MySQL, PostgreSQL, and SQL Server default to an autocommit mode in which each statement you execute is treated as a transaction in and of itself. (Thus, you cannot roll back a statement when the result isn't what you expected).

You can disable autocommit in SQL Server with the following statement:

```
SET IMPLICIT_TRANSACTIONS ON
```

You can enable autocommit again using:

```
SET IMPLICIT_TRANSACTIONS OFF
```

You leave SQL Server's and PostgreSQL's autocommit mode whenever you issue an explicit BEGIN TRANSACTION (SQL Server) or BEGIN (PostgreSQL) statement. See "Starting a Transaction" below for details.

In MySQL, you can disable autocommit with:

```
SET AUTOCOMMIT=0
```

And you can enable it again with:

```
SET AUTOCOMMIT=1
```

You automatically leave autocommit mode whenever you issue a BEGIN or BEGIN WORK statement.

Starting a Transaction: DB2

DB2 does not implement an SQL statement to explicitly begin a transaction. When you connect and issue an SQL statement, you begin a transaction. You also begin a transaction with the first SQL statement following a COMMIT.

Starting a Transaction: MySQL

Use START TRANSACTION to begin a MySQL transaction explicitly (when using any version prior to MySQL 4.0.11, use BEGIN or BEGIN WORK). When not in autocommit mode, any SQL statement you issue will begin a new transaction implicitly.

WARNING

Only certain types of MySQL tables (InnoDB tables, for example) support transactions. Changes to data in non-transactional tables take place immediately and permanently, regardless of whether you are in a transaction.

Before beginning a transaction, you can use SET TRANSACTION to change the transaction isolation level. A reasonable sequence of statements might then be:

```
SET [GLOBAL|SESSION] TRANSACTION ISOLATION LEVEL
    {READ UNCOMMITTED|READ COMMITTED
    |REPEATABLE READ|SERIALIZABLE};
START TRANSACTION;
```

By default, SET TRANSACTION sets the isolation level only for your next transaction. Use SET SESSION TRANSACTION to set the default isolation level for your entire session.

Starting a Transaction: Oracle

Within Oracle, for all practical purposes, you're always in a transaction. The first SQL statement you execute after you connect begins an implicit transaction, as does the first SQL statement you execute following the end of a transaction. Oracle's default transaction type is read/write with statement-level read consistency.

You can begin a transaction using SET TRANSACTION explicitly:

```
SET TRANSACTION options [NAME 'tran_name']
options ::=
   {READ {ONLY|WRITE}
   |ISOLATION LEVEL {SERIALIZABLE|READ COMMITTED}
   |USE ROLLBACK SEGMENT segment_name
```

The options and parameters are as follows:

NAME 'tran_name'

Specifies a name of up to 255 bytes for the transaction. Upon COMMIT, the name will be saved as the transaction comment, overriding any COMMIT comment. It's especially helpful to name distributed transactions.

READ ONLY

Gives you a read-only transaction that does not "see" any changes committed after the transaction begins.

READ WRITE

Gives you the default transaction type: a read/write transaction with statement-level read consistency.

ISOLATION LEVEL SERIALIZABLE

Gives you a read/write serializable transaction, as defined in the SQL standard.

ISOLATION LEVEL READ COMMITTED

Gives you the default Oracle transaction behavior, but using ANSI/ISO SQL syntax.

```
USE ROLLBACK SEGMENT segment_name
```
Creates a default transaction and assigns it to the specified rollback segment. (Obsolete; use automatic undo management instead.)

Here are some example SET TRANSACTION statements:

```
SET TRANSACTION READ ONLY;

SET TRANSACTION ISOLATION LEVEL SERIALIZABLE;

SET TRANSACTION
    ISOLATION LEVEL READ COMMITTED;
    NAME 'Delete all attractions';
```

If you name a distributed transaction and that transaction fails, its name will appear in the DBA_2PC_PENDING table's TRAN_COMMENT column.

Starting a Transaction: PostgreSQL

To start a PostgreSQL transaction, issue a BEGIN command, which takes PostgreSQL out of autocommit mode. The syntax for PostgreSQL 8.0 and higher is:

```
BEGIN [WORK|TRANSACTION] [iso_mode|mode_iso]
iso_mode ::= isolation [[,] mode]
mode_iso ::= mode [[,] isolation]
isolation ::= ISOLATION LEVEL
               {SERIALIZABLE|REPEATABLE READ
               |READ COMMITTED|READ UNCOMMITTED}
mode ::= {READ WRITE|READ ONLY}
```

For example:

```
BEGIN ISOLATION LEVEL READ COMMITTED, READ WRITE;
```

In this syntax, you can use the keyword START instead of BEGIN. Also, you can separate isolation and mode using either whitespace or a comma. The default isolation and mode are READ COMMITTED and READ WRITE, respectively.

In PostgreSQL 7.4 and earlier, BEGIN syntax was simply:

```
BEGIN [WORK|TRANSACTION]
```

Next, to set transaction characteristics, you can follow the BEGIN statement immediately with a SET TRANSACTION statement:

```
SET TRANSACTION [iso_mode|mode_iso]
```

For example:

```
BEGIN;
SET TRANSACTION READ WRITE;
```

Finally, you can set the default isolation and mode for a session by using the following command:

```
SET SESSION CHARACTERISTICS AS TRANSACTION
    [iso_mode|mode_iso]
```

Starting a Transaction: SQL Server

Use the following statement to begin an SQL Server transaction explicitly:

```
BEGIN TRAN[SACTION]
    [[transaction_name]
    [WITH MARK ['description']]]
```

Transaction names are limited to 32 characters. You can specify a name by means of a variable, as in @variable.

Use the WITH MARK clause to note a transaction in the database log; you can also specify a *description* for it if you wish.

To begin a distributed transaction, use:

```
BEGIN DISTRIBUTED TRAN[SACTION]
    [transaction_name]
```

As with BEGIN TRANSACTION, you can specify the transaction name by means of a variable in the form @variable.

SQL Server's default isolation level is READ COMMITTED. Before beginning a transaction, use the following statement to specify the isolation level of your choice:

```
SET TRANSACTION ISOLATION LEVEL
    {READ COMMITTED|READ UNCOMMITTED
    |REPEATABLE READ|SERIALIZABLE}
```

This statement sets the isolation level to be used for all subsequent transactions in your session.

Ending a Transaction

To end a transaction and make the transaction's changes permanent, issue a COMMIT statement:

```
COMMIT [WORK]
```

Oracle supports an optional COMMENT clause:

```
COMMIT [WORK] [COMMENT 'text']
```

WORK is an optional word allowed by the ISO SQL standard (but not supported by MySQL), and it is commonly omitted. In Oracle, any name you specify using SET TRANSACTION when you begin a transaction overrides any comment you specify when you commit that transaction.

SQL Server also supports a COMMIT TRANSACTION statement, which enables you to identify the transaction you want to commit:

```
COMMIT TRAN[SACTION] [transaction_name]
```

SQL Server actually ignores any *transaction_name* that you specify. It allows a name only to make it easier for you to associate nested COMMITs with their corresponding BEGIN TRANSACTION statements.

Oracle supports the following syntax to force a distributed transaction to commit:

```
COMMIT [WORK] FORCE
    {'local_tran_id'|'global_tran_id'}
    [system_change_number]
```

You identify a distributed transaction using either its local or global transaction ID, which you can obtain from the DBA_2PC_PENDING view. You have the option of assigning a system change number (SCN) or defaulting to the current SCN.

Aborting a Transaction

To abort a transaction, use the ROLLBACK statement:

```
ROLLBACK [WORK]
```

As with COMMIT, the word WORK (which is not supported by MySQL) is commonly omitted. When you ROLLBACK a transaction, you undo all of that transaction's changes.

SQL Server also supports a ROLLBACK TRANSACTION statement, which enables you to specify the name of the transaction to roll back:

```
ROLLBACK TRAN[SACTION] [transaction_name]
```

By default, ROLLBACK TRANSACTION rolls back the current transaction. In a nested transaction, that means the innermost transaction. If you specify a transaction name, you *must* specify the outermost transaction. That transaction and all nested transactions are then undone.

Oracle supports the following syntax to force a distributed transaction to roll back:

```
ROLLBACK [WORK] FORCE
    {'local_tran_id'|'global_tran_id'}
```

You identify a distributed transaction using either its local or global transaction ID, which you can obtain from the DBA_2PC_PENDING view.

Aborting to a Savepoint

Rather than rolling back an entire transaction, you can roll back only part of one. To do this, you must have marked points in the transaction, known as *savepoints*, which are specified using the following syntax for MySQL, Oracle, and PostgreSQL:

```
SAVEPOINT savepoint_name
```

For DB2, you can specify:

```
SAVEPOINT savepoint_name [UNIQUE]
    ON ROLLBACK RETAIN CURSORS
    [ON ROLLBACK RETAIN LOCKS]
```

For SQL Server, you can specify:

```
SAVE TRAN[SACTION] savepoint_name
```

You can then ROLLBACK to any of those savepoints using:

```
ROLLBACK [WORK] TO savepoint_name
```

Except in DB2, you must use:

```
ROLLBACK TO SAVEPOINT savepoint_name
```

The following is an example from Oracle:

```
SET TRANSACTION ISOLATION LEVEL READ COMMITTED;
UPDATE township SET name = UPPER(name);
SAVEPOINT name_upper_cased;
DELETE FROM trip;
ROLLBACK TO name_upper_cased;
COMMIT;
```

The net effect of this transaction is to set all township names to uppercase. The DELETE against the **trip** table is undone by the ROLLBACK TO the savepoint that was established following the UPDATE statement.

Union Queries

Union queries use keywords such as UNION, EXCEPT (MINUS in Oracle), and INTERSECT to "combine" results from two or more queries in useful ways.

UNION and UNION ALL

Use the UNION keyword to combine results from two SELECT statements into one result set. (Think of stacking the rows from two result sets.) Any duplicate rows are eliminated from the final results, unless you specify UNION ALL to preserve them.

NOTE

Some would argue that you should use UNION ALL when you *know* for a certainty that no duplicates are possible, thus improving performance by avoiding the sort.

UNION

The UNION operator conforms closely to SQL's origin in set theory. It is used to combine two rowsets and remove any duplicates from the results. For example:

```
SELECT u.id, u.name
FROM upfall u
WHERE open_to_public = 'y'
UNION
SELECT u.id, u.name
FROM upfall u
JOIN owner o ON u.owner_id = o.id
WHERE o.type = 'public';
```

This query lists waterfalls that are either open to the public or that are owned by a public entity (such as a national park). Duplicate elimination ensures that even if a waterfall fits into both categories (is both open to the public *and* owned by a public entity), it is returned only once in the query's result set.

NOTE

Duplicate elimination requires overhead, generally in the form of a limited sort operation. If you don't need duplicate elimination, you'll get better performance with UNION ALL.

UNION ALL

UNION ALL is UNION without the duplicate elimination. The following UNION ALL query simulates an outer join, with **upfall** as the required table and **owner** as the optional table. The first SELECT picks up waterfalls that *can* join to **owner**, whereas the second SELECT picks up those falls with no known owner:

```
SELECT u1.name AS fall, o.name AS owner
FROM upfall u1 JOIN owner o ON u1.owner_id = o.id
UNION ALL
SELECT u2.name AS fall, 'Unknown' AS owner
FROM upfall u2
WHERE u2.owner_id IS NULL;
```

Getting correct results from this query depends on a foreign key integrity constraint to ensure that any non-null value in **upfall.owner_id** references an existing row in **owner**. Without such a constraint, the second SELECT must be written to include rows with invalid **owner_id** values.

ORDER BY in Union Queries

SQL allows only one ORDER BY clause per query. In a union query, the ORDER BY clause belongs at the very end:

```
SELECT u.id, u.name
FROM upfall u
WHERE open_to_public = 'y'
UNION
SELECT u.id, u.name
```

```
FROM upfall u
JOIN owner o ON u.owner_id = o.id
WHERE o.type = 'public'
ORDER BY name;
```

The sorting operation then applies to the collective results from all SELECT expressions involved in the union.

Names and Data Types in a Union

The column names used for the first SELECT in a union query become the names of their respective result columns. In the following query, the columns will be named col_a and col_b:

```
SELECT 'One' col_a, 'Two' col_b FROM dual
UNION
SELECT 'Three', 'Four' FROM dual;
```

Also be aware that column data types must correspond. For example, don't try to perform a union of a numeric column to a text column without first writing an explicit conversion to synchronize the data types.

NOTE

Remember, PostgreSQL requires the AS keyword when specifying column aliases (e.g., 'One' AS col_a).

Order of Evaluation

When writing a statement with multiple UNION operations, you can use parentheses to specify the order in which the union operations occur in all platforms except MySQL. The following is a contrived example (to run it in Oracle, replace EXCEPT with MINUS):

```
SELECT * FROM upfall
EXCEPT
(SELECT * FROM upfall
 UNION
 SELECT * FROM upfall);
```

The first SELECT returns all rows from upfall. The UNION of the two SELECTs in parentheses also returns all rows from upfall. When you subtract all rows from all rows, you have none left. Thus, as written, the query returns no rows. If you remove the parentheses, however, you'll get all upfall rows in the result set.

NOTE

Unless you specify otherwise, union operations are performed in top-down order, except that INTERSECT takes precedence over UNION and EXCEPT.

EXCEPT (or MINUS) and EXCEPT ALL

Use the EXCEPT union operation (MINUS in Oracle) to "subtract" the results of one query from another. If you do not need duplicate elimination, use EXCEPT ALL. Note that MySQL does not support EXCEPT.

EXCEPT (MINUS in Oracle)

To find all owners without waterfalls, you can subtract the list of owners *with* falls from the total list of owners:

```
SELECT o.id FROM owner o
EXCEPT
SELECT u.owner_id FROM upfall u;
```

Remember that you must use the MINUS keyword rather than EXCEPT to run this query in Oracle.

EXCEPT ALL

DB2 and PostgreSQL support EXCEPT ALL. The following query uses that operation to return a list of owners who have at least two waterfalls:

```
SELECT u.owner_id FROM upfall u
EXCEPT ALL
SELECT o.id FROM owner o;
```

The first SELECT will potentially return many IDs per owner (one from each fall that is owned), whereas the second SELECT will return exactly one ID for each owner. Owners with two or more falls will have their IDs listed two or more times in the results of the first query. In the case of Pictured Rocks, the resulting subtraction looks like this:

```
1
1
1
EXCEPT ALL
1
```

Because EXCEPT ALL is used, the single owner ID from the owner table is subtracted from the three from the upfall table, which leaves two occurrences in the final result set:

```
1
1
```

Because the EXCEPT operation still requires some sorting of the results to perform the subtraction operation, using EXCEPT ALL may not produce the same kind of performance boost you get from using UNION ALL instead of UNION.

INTERSECT and INTERSECT ALL

The INTERSECT operation is used to find rows in common between the result sets of two SELECTs. Use INTERSECT ALL when you do not want duplicate elimination. Note that MySQL does not support INTERSECT.

INTERSECT

The following INTERSECT query is similar to the query used to illustrate UNION. In this example, rather than being an "either/or" query, the query returns falls that are both open to the public *and* owned by a private (not public this time) organization:

```
SELECT u.id, u.name
FROM upfall u
WHERE open_to_public = 'y'
```

```
INTERSECT
SELECT u.id, u.name
FROM upfall u
JOIN owner o ON u.owner_id = o.id
WHERE o.type = 'private';
```

Some kind of sorting or hashing operation will be executed to find rows in common between the two result sets. Duplicate elimination ensures that each fall is returned only once.

INTERSECT ALL

Use INTERSECT ALL when you want to consider duplicates. Only DB2 and PostgreSQL support this. For example, given the following data:

```
MARQUETTE
MARQUETTE
BARAGA
BARAGA
MUNISING
INTERSECT ALL
MARQUETTE
MARQUETTE
BARAGA
```

INTERSECT will yield:

```
MARQUETTE
BARAGA
```

whereas INTERSECT ALL will yield:

```
MARQUETTE
MARQUETTE
BARAGA
```

Because Marquette appears twice in both result sets, it appears twice in the final results. Baraga, on the other hand, appears only once in the second result set, so it appears just once in the final result set.

Updating Data

To modify existing data in a table, use the UPDATE statement. You can update one row or many rows, you can specify a single set of new values in the statement, or you can generate new values through a subquery.

Simple Updates

A simple UPDATE takes the following form:

```
UPDATE table
SET column = value, column = value ...
WHERE predicates
```

In this form, *predicates* identifies one or more rows that you want to update. You can specify as many *column = value* pairs as you like—one for each column you want to modify:

```
UPDATE upfall
SET owner_id = 1
WHERE name = 'Munising Falls';
```

When you specify only one new value, you will usually want to update only one row, and your WHERE-clause predicates should reference primary or unique key values to identify that row. Using expressions, you can write sensible UPDATEs that modify many rows. The following example works in DB2:

```
UPDATE upfall
SET datum = UPPER(datum),
    lat_lon = TRIM(UPPER(lat_lon));
```

This example also demonstrates the use of the comma to separate multiple-column updates in a SET clause.

NOTE

In MySQL, if you are updating a self-referential foreign key or its related primary key, you should include an ORDER BY clause at the end of your update to control the order in which rows are updated. For more on this issue, see "Deleting in Order" on page 47 and "Subquery Inserts" on page 69.

New Values from a Subquery

You can also generate new values from a subquery. One way to do this is to write separate subqueries for each column that you are updating:

```
UPDATE table
SET column = (subquery), column = (subquery), ...
```

For example (note that PostgreSQL and SQL Server do not allow the table alias u):

```
UPDATE upfall u
SET owner_id =
    (SELECT o.id FROM owner o
     WHERE o.name = 'Pictured Rocks')
WHERE u.name = 'Miners Falls';
```

Such subqueries must always return zero or one row and one column. If zero rows are returned, then the value is set to null.

In DB2 and Oracle, you can also write a subquery that returns more than one column value, in which case the number of values returned must correspond to the columns you are updating:

```
UPDATE table
SET (column, column, ...) = (subquery)
```

For example, to update names and descriptions with any new information in the new_falls table (see the section "Merging Data" on page 86 for a better way to do this), specify:

```
UPDATE upfall u
SET (u.name, u.description) =
    (SELECT nf.name, nf.description
```

```
        FROM new_falls nf
        WHERE u.id = nf.id)
    WHERE u.id IN (SELECT nf2.id
                    FROM new_falls nf2);
```

Be careful with this kind of update. If you omit the WHERE clause in this query, all rows in **upfall** will be updated, regardless of whether corresponding rows exist in **new_falls**. Worse, **upfall**'s **name** and **description** columns will be set to null in cases where no corresponding **new_falls** rows exist.

Updating Views and Subqueries

All platforms allow UPDATEs to run against views. DB2 and Oracle also allow updates to run against subqueries (i.e., inline views):

```
UPDATE (SELECT * FROM upfall
        WHERE owner_id IS NULL)
SET open_to_public = 'n';
```

PostgreSQL does not support updates to inline views. PostgreSQL requires any view that is the target of an UPDATE statement to be associated with an ON UPDATE DO INSTEAD rule.

Database systems place various restrictions on the updating of views, but in general, you must be able to access unambiguously a single table row from a given view row in order to issue an update against that view (or subquery).

UPDATE FROM Clause

PostgreSQL and SQL Server let you write a FROM clause in an UPDATE statement in order to gather columns from multiple tables to use in your SET expressions. For example, the following statement works in SQL Server and appends the owner type from the owner table to each waterfall's description:

```
UPDATE upfall
    SET description
        = u.description + ' (' + o.type + ')'
```

```
FROM upfall u JOIN owner o
ON u.owner_id = o.id;
```

When using this syntax, you must ensure that the UPDATE is *deterministic*, meaning that there is only one possible value for any column you reference in a SET expression. The join condition in this query accomplishes this—there will always be only one owner per waterfall.

Notice the use of aliases in the SET clause. The first reference to **description** is unqualified. The column name you specify following the SET keyword must be in the table that is the target of the UPDATE statement. The second occurrence of **description**, however, *is* qualified. All values feeding into the update must come from the tables listed in the FROM clause.

Returning Updated Data: DB2

DB2 allows you to query the before and after values from rows affected by an UPDATE statement. Simply SELECT from that UPDATE statement. For example:

```
SELECT * FROM NEW TABLE (
    UPDATE gov_unit
    SET name = UPPER(name)
    WHERE MOD(id,2) = 0
);
```

Specify FROM NEW TABLE to see the newly updated values. Specify FROM OLD TABLE to see the original values. Be sure to wrap your UPDATE in parentheses.

Returning Updated Data: Oracle

You can use Oracle's RETURNING clause to return values that you update. Here is the syntax:

```
UPDATE ...
SET ...
WHERE ...
RETURNING expression [,expression ...]
INTO variable [,variable ...]
```

If you update a single row, Oracle expects to return values into bind variables; if you update more than one row, it expects to return values into bind arrays. See "Returning Deleted Data: Oracle" on page 50 for an example involving arrays and "Returning Inserted Values: Oracle" on page 70 for a single-row example.

Returning Updated Data: SQL Server

You can use SQL Server's OUTPUT clause to return values from newly inserted rows. For example:

```
UPDATE gov_unit
SET type = UPPER(type)
OUTPUT INSERTED.id,
       INSERTED.type AS new_type,
       DELETED.type AS old_type;
```

Specify INSERTED to reference post-update values. Specify DELETED to reference pre-update values. The preceding query displays both old and new type values as follows:

```
id          new_type old_type
----------- -------- --------
1           CITY     City
2           COUNTY   County
3           STATE    State
...
```

You can use the syntax INSERTED.* or DELETED.* to return all post- and pre-update values respectively. You can specify expressions such as LOWER(INSERTED.type). You can specify column aliases as in any query, with or without the optional AS keyword.

Window Functions

Window functions enable you to look at different levels of aggregation in the same result row. They make it easy to specify cumulative sum, moving average, share-of, and many other important calculations. Window functions are supported in Oracle (where they are known as *analytic functions*), DB2 (where they are called *OLAP functions*), SQL Server, and PostgreSQL.

Defining a Summary Window

The defining role of a window function is to specify a *window*, or partition of rows, over which the function operates. You specify a window using the `OVER ( . . . )` clause, which you can apply to any of the aggregate functions listed in Table 6 (under "Grouping and Summarizing" on page 52). For example:

```
SELECT
    u.id, u.county_id, u.northing n1,
    MIN(u.northing) OVER (PARTITION BY u.county_id) n2,
    AVG(u.northing) OVER () n3,
    MAX(u.northing) OVER (PARTITION BY u.open_to_public) n4
FROM upfall u;
```

Each row returned by this query will have the following four **northing** values:

n1

> The northing value for the waterfall described by the current row

n2

> The lowest northing value of any waterfall in the same county

n3

> The average northing value of all waterfalls

n4

> The highest northing value of any waterfall having the same "open to public" status

An OVER() clause with nothing between the parentheses simply denotes an aggregate function's use as a window function. No GROUP BY clause is necessary, and the specified summary value is returned in each detail row. The summary comprises all rows in the result set.

To gain the effect of a GROUP BY, add a PARTITION BY clause within the OVER() clause. The `PARTITION BY u.county_id` in the example partitions detail rows into groups based on their `county_id` values. The `MIN(u.northing)` function is applied to each group. Each detail row is then returned with a copy of the `MIN(u.northing)` function's result for that row's group.

The example query in this section returns data at a variety of summary levels. First, you have the detail—one row for each fall. Each of those rows then contains data summarized by county, by the entire result set, and by "open to public" status.

You can partition by more than one column; for example:

```
MAX(u.northing) OVER (
    PARTITION BY u.county_id,
                 u.open_to_public)
```

Ordering and Ranking Within a Window

You can sort the rows within each partition by placing an ORDER BY clause within the OVER() clause. After you've sorted the rows, you can rank them in various ways. For example, the following query ranks the northernness of each waterfall in three different ways with respect to other falls in the same county that have the same "open to public" status:

```
SELECT
    u.id, u.county_id, u.open_to_public, u.name,
    ROW_NUMBER() OVER (
        PARTITION BY u.county_id, u.open_to_public
        ORDER BY northing DESC) r1,
    RANK() OVER (
        PARTITION BY u.county_id, u.open_to_public
        ORDER BY northing DESC) r2,
    DENSE_RANK() OVER (
        PARTITION BY u.county_id, u.open_to_public
        ORDER BY northing DESC) r3,
    u.northing
FROM upfall u
WHERE u.northing IS NOT NULL;
```

The following output showing the ranking of publicly accessible waterfalls in Alger County illustrates the three different ranking approaches:

```
...NAME              R1   R2   R3   NORTHING
...--------------- ---- ---- ---- ---------
...Munising Falls    1    1    1   5141184
...Twin Falls #1     2    2    2   5140500
...Twin Falls #2     3    2    2   5140500
...Tannery Falls     4    4    3   5140000
...
```

The `ORDER BY northing DESC` clause sorts the rows within each window in descending order by `northing`. (This sorting is conceptual and may be optimized away by your database platform.) The three functions, ROW_NUMBER(), RANK(), and DENSE_RANK(), then apply their ranking logic to the rows of each window as follows:

`ROW_NUMBER()`

> Applies a sequentially increasing number to each row in a window. This is evident in column `R1` of the result set. The northernmost row will be number 1, the next northernmost row will be number 2, and so forth.

`RANK()`

> Returns the same result as ROW_NUMBER(), except that when two rows have the same `northing` value, they will be given the same rank. This is why Twin Falls #1 and #2 are both ranked in the number 2 position (column `R2` in the result set). RANK() will then skip values to ensure that the rank assigned to a given row is always one greater than the number of rows that are ranked lower. For this reason, Tannery Falls is ranked at number 4—it occupies the fourth position.

`DENSE_RANK()`

> Does not skip values. Compare the results from RANK() in column `R2` with those of DENSE_RANK() in column `R3`. In both cases, Twin Falls #1 and #2 tie for the number 2 position. In the case of DENSE_RANK(), however, Tan-

nery Falls is treated as though it occupies the *third* position, not the fourth.

There is no particular "right way" to rank. Choose the method that delivers the results that work best in your application.

NOTE

You don't need to specify a PARTITION BY clause in front of an ORDER BY. For example, `RANK() OVER (ORDER BY northing DESC)` will rank the current row's northing against all rows in the query's result set.

Comparing Values Across Rows

DB2, Oracle, PostgreSQL, and SQL Server implement some functions that are quite useful for comparing values across row boundaries. LAG and LEAD allow you to look ahead and behind a specified number of rows. FIRST_VALUE and LAST_VALUE return values from the first and last rows in a window, respectively. NTH_VALUE (Oracle only) lets you return a value from a specific row in a window by specifying that row's number.

The following query runs in Oracle. Remove the NTH_VALUE invocation to run on the other platforms.

```
SELECT
    u.id, u.county_id,
    u.northing n1,
    FIRST_VALUE(u.northing) OVER (
        PARTITION BY u.county_id
        ORDER BY northing DESC) n2,
    LAG(u.northing, 1, 9999999) OVER (
        PARTITION BY u.county_id
        ORDER BY northing DESC) n3,
    LEAD(u.northing, 1, 0) OVER (
        PARTITION BY u.county_id
        ORDER BY northing DESC) n4,
    LAST_VALUE(u.northing) OVER (
        PARTITION BY u.county_id
        ORDER BY northing DESC) n5,
```

```
    NTH_VALUE(u.northing, 2)
        IGNORE NULLS OVER (
        PARTITION BY u.county_id
        ORDER BY northing DESC) N6
  FROM upfall u;
```

The LAG and LEAD functions each take three arguments. The first argument is a value in which you are interested. The second argument is a numeric row offset. The third argument is a default value to return when there is no row at the specified offset.

The LAG function in this example returns u.northing from the preceding row in the same window (i.e., for the same county) when it is sorted in descending order by northing.

Oracle's NTH_VALUE function takes two arguments: the value to return and the row number from which to retrieve that value. The IGNORE NULLS clause is optional. RESPECT NULLS is the default. You can also specify FROM FIRST or FROM LAST preceding the IGNORE NULLS clause, to specify whether to count from the beginning or the end of the window.

NOTE

It is not necessary for all window functions in a given query to PARTITION BY or ORDER BY the same set of columns as in this section's example. The window and sorting criteria can be different in each function.

The six northing values returned by the preceding query are as follows:

n1

> The northing for the waterfall described by the current row.

n2

> The highest northing of all waterfalls in the same county.

n3

The next highest northing for the county, or 9,999,999 if no higher value exists in the same window. LAG sounds as though it should return the next lower northing, but the descending sort turns that around.

n4

The next lower northing for the county, or 0 if no lower value exists in the same window. See the entry for n3 for the effect of the descending sort.

n5

The lowest northing of all waterfalls in the same county.

n6

The northing for the waterfall described by the second row in the window.

LAG and LEAD can be very useful, but only when the same offset applies consistently to each row, and only when you have sorted your windows (i.e., the rows in each window) in some meaningful order.

Summarizing over a Moving Window

Within a partition (keeping in mind that the entire rowset can be considered a partition), you can choose to summarize over a moving window of rows. DB2 and Oracle implement this functionality. For example, you might choose to return the MIN and MAX northing values within 1000 meters of each waterfall. Here's how you might accomplish that:

```
SELECT u.id, u.county_id, u.northing n1,
    MIN(u.northing) OVER (
        ORDER BY u.northing
        RANGE BETWEEN 1000 PRECEDING
                  AND 1000 FOLLOWING) n2,
    MAX(u.northing) OVER (
        ORDER BY u.northing
        RANGE BETWEEN 1000 PRECEDING
                  AND 1000 FOLLOWING) n3
FROM upfall u
WHERE u.northing IS NOT NULL;
```

In this particular example, there is only one partition—the entire rowset. You could easily add `PARTITION BY u.county_id` to restrict the MIN and MAX computations to each current waterfall's county.

The RANGE BETWEEN clause in this example is considered a *framing clause*. Framing clause syntax is complex, and it varies between vendors.

Window Function Evaluation and Placement

In the scheme of SQL processing, window functions are among the last elements to be evaluated. They follow any WHERE, GROUP BY, and HAVING clause processing, and they precede ORDER BY. Thus, you can only place window functions in the SELECT list and ORDER BY clauses of a query.

Index

We'd like to hear your suggestions for improving our indexes. Send email to
index@oreilly.com.

CPSIA information can be obtained
at www.ICGtesting.com
Printed in the USA
BVOW10s2051310317
479992BV00006B/7/P